Sister Thea Bowman

Sister Thea Bowman

Do You Hear Me, Church?

Peggy A. Sklar

Paulist Press
New York / Mahwah, NJ

Cover image: Portrait by Anthony VanArsdale. Used with permission of the National Black Catholic Congress.

Cover design by Sharyn Banks
Book design by Lynn Else

Library of Congress Cataloging-in-Publication Data
Names: Sklar, Peggy A., author.
Title: Sister Thea Bowman : do you hear me, Church? / Peggy A Sklar.
Description: New York : Paulist Press, [2020] | Summary: "Sister Thea Bowman: Do You Hear Me, Church? is a biography for young adult readers. Sr. Bowman (1937–1990) was an educator, evangelist, gifted singer, scholar, and advocate for diversity and the inclusion of African Americans and African American culture in the Catholic Church"—Provided by publisher.
Identifiers: LCCN 2019029194 (print) | LCCN 2019029195 (ebook) | ISBN 9780809167920 (paperback) | ISBN 9781587688744 (ebook)
Subjects: LCSH: Bowman, Thea. | African American Catholics—Biography—Juvenile literature.
Classification: LCC BX4705.B8113 S55 2020 (print) | LCC BX4705.B8113 (ebook) | DDC 271/.97302 [B]—dc23
LC record available at https://lccn.loc.gov/2019029194
LC ebook record available at https://lccn.loc.gov/2019029195

ISBN 978-0-8091-6792-0 (paperback)
ISBN 978-1-58768-874-4 (e-book)

Published by Paulist Press
997 Macarthur Boulevard
Mahwah, New Jersey 07430
www.paulistpress.com

Printed and bound in the
United States of America

To my grandmother, who shared a name
and a *joie de vivre* with Sister Thea

———————————————————

To my mother, who taught me to love reading

I think the difference between me and some people is that I'm content to do my little bit. Sometimes people think they have to do great things in order to make change. But if each person would light a candle, we'd have a tremendous light.

Servant of God Sister Thea Bowman, FSPA
60 Minutes Interview

CONTENTS

FOREWORD

When we fall into this book, being drawn deep into the life of Sister Thea Bowman, FSPA, PhD, we are guided along a journey that will be filled with grace, wonder, and awe. The author presents a fascinating biography of one of God's most precious gifts to our Church and to our country. Sister Thea Bowman, we are told, challenged by a sickness that would eventually claim her earthly life, displayed the courage of a woman whose horizon was infinite, and she said, "I'm going to live until I die." This book allows us to feel her vibrant and challenging spirit even after her death.

I experienced Sister Thea's vibrant spirit when we taught at the Institute for Black Catholic Studies at Xavier University in New Orleans, beginning in 1986. At times we team-taught classes and at others we presented together at conferences.

On July 4, 1989, Sister Thea met Institute participants in her home parish in Canton, Mississippi, and made what would be her last singing performance. Earlier in the day she had been undergoing radiation therapy for her cancer. When she was wheeled into the assembly, the air changed. After selected faculty and students sang, told stories, and recited poetry, Sister Thea asked for the microphone. Visibly drained from the therapy session, weak in body but strong in spirit, she said, "I know you all want me to sing something, don't you?" Then, gathering power from somewhere deep inside the room, she began to sing, "Done made my vow to the Lord, and I never will turn back. I will go, I shall go, to see what the end will be."

When we finish reading this great gift from Peggy Sklar, we are blessed by the final words of the book, which also serve as the title: "Do you hear me, Church?" This biography proves that we can still hear the voice of Sister Thea, can still be instructed by her in how to form a real church—a church in which everybody has a seat in the kingdom—a church where there is no time limit, no end. Thea Bowman broke through every barrier she ever confronted: a devoted daughter, a beloved friend, a charismatic teacher, a multidisciplinary scholar, a community builder, and a prophet sent by the ancestors to teach us what we must learn in order to be ready for the future.

Many preachers will shout out during a sermon, "Can I get a witness?" Peggy Sklar has done a great service with this well-written and deeply felt book: she has given us a witness. Sister Thea Bowman made her vow to the Lord, and we are all still being guided by her light.

This book is a sacrament of confirmation.

Joseph A. Brown, SJ, PhD
Professor of Africana Studies at
Southern Illinois University, Carbondale
Author of *A Retreat with Thea Bowman and*
Bede Abram: Leaning on the Lord
(Franciscan Media, 1997)

PREFACE

Sister Thea Bowman, FSPA, was an extraordinary person who made enormous contributions to the fields of education and social justice. Born to a Protestant family in a small, segregated community in the Deep South, Sister Thea Bowman embraced the Catholic Church as a child because of the good works performed by the Church's ministers. It is impossible to separate the story of Sister Thea from the racial injustices of her time. As an adult, she challenged the Church to see that all people, regardless of race or culture, could not only live and work together in harmony, but worship together as well. She showed us what it truly means to be a "catholic," or universal, Church.

Sister Thea was an outstanding student, teacher, and scholar. She was a dynamic presenter and talented vocalist. She was also committed to religious life in the Franciscan tradition that she had chosen. She maintained a deep and loving relationship with her parents and family. The life of Sister Thea shows us that God continues to be active in our lives and calls people to service in the Church from all walks of life. Sister Thea answered God's call, and like St. Francis of Assisi, she sought to bring light where there is darkness.

Young people played an important part in Sister

Thea's life. She loved teaching and brought enormous spirit to her classroom by making the subject matter captivating to her students. She encouraged children and youth to realize their full potential. Sister Thea believed that they must understand that "you're somebody special 'cause you're God's child." This message is especially important today, when children and youth are subjected to so many outside forces, particularly social media, where they often derive their self-esteem. Sister Thea believed that if children and youth recognized how truly special they are, they might be better protected from the negative influences that surround them and be able to live out their calling, just as she had.

ACKNOWLEDGMENTS

I am very grateful to the people I met in Mississippi who knew Sister Thea and shared their memories and stories with me. My research was made possible with the assistance of the Canton Multicultural Center and Museum, Holy Child Jesus Church, and the Diocese of Jackson. I will always remember the kindness and generosity of the people I met in Mississippi. In addition, the Viterbo University Archives provided valuable assistance. I wish to thank the Franciscan Sisters of Perpetual Adoration for patiently answering my questions to assist in ensuring accuracy and helping me to understand convent life, particularly in the early 1950s.

I am in particular awe of the early sisters, brothers, and priests who worked so hard for the people they served in Mississippi. It is difficult to fathom the conditions under which many of them ministered. Their efforts in social justice and in bringing the gospel to others made a difference in the lives of so many people.

Chapter 1
THE BEGINNING

"Mama, Mama! Where are you? Come quickly! The dog has run off. Oh, Mama. What will we do?" The crying girl stood grief-stricken as her little white dog bounded down the street. Crossing the street, the dog headed straight for one of the houses on the other side of the road.

Bertha's mother, hearing the wailing girl, appeared and without hesitation dashed out the door, her housecoat flapping in the wind behind her. Mrs. Bowman, normally a proper and refined woman, ignored the fact that she was not suitably dressed to go out, and ran after the runaway dog.

Wearing a housecoat outside was the very least of Mrs. Bowman's problems that day. Her daughter's beloved pet had not only crossed the street but had run to the white side of the road. The Bowmans, an African American family, lived on the black side. This was the 1940s in Canton, Mississippi, in the heart of the American South. In this neighborhood, whites lived on one side of the street while African Americans lived on the other. Though it might have looked like one neighborhood on a map, the two sides of the road were very different.

Rules were rules and it did not matter that the Bowmans were professionals. Bertha's father was a doctor and her mother was a former school teacher, like her own mother. Education was of no consequence; all that mattered in the segregated society of that time was the color of their skin and that they followed the rules whether just or not. Educated African Americans still had to remember their place in the society in which they lived.

Bertha Elizabeth Bowman was born December 29, 1937, in Yazoo City, Mississippi, to Mary Esther (Coleman) and Theon Edward Bowman. Young Bertha was named for her paternal aunt, Bertha C. Bowman. Yazoo City was part of the Mississippi Delta and about thirty-three miles west of her parents' home in Canton in central Mississippi. The unusual name, Yazoo City, is derived from the Yazoo River, which was named for a small extinct Native American tribe. At one time, there were many Native American tribes in the state. Today, the Mississippi Band of Choctaw Indians, numbering ten thousand members, is the only federally recognized tribe. The names of numerous Mississippi counties, towns, and rivers are of Native American origin, including the state name itself, which comes from the Mississippi River and means "father of waters."

Bertha's father had also been born in Yazoo City, but moved with his family to Memphis, Tennessee, as a child. At the time of Mrs. Bowman's pregnancy, Yazoo City offered better medical care for an African American woman than Canton, particularly for an older woman having her first child. Canton had no hospitals that would treat African Americans. Knowing the complications that could occur, Dr. Bowman wanted to make sure that his wife had the best medical care available to her. But even the best of plans can go awry, as Mrs. Bowman went into early labor at the home of the family friend where she was staying in Yazoo City. After being notified of her labor, Dr. Bowman arrived before his wife's doctor and delivered his own daughter.

The infant Bertha would come home to her parents' house in Canton. The Bowmans lived at 136 Hill Street in what is known as a "shotgun house," a one-story long, narrow residence with a front and back door, built around the turn of the twentieth century. A shotgun house is typically found in the South, and the name comes from the fact that one could shoot from the front door straight through the house to the back door. Some historians believe that the more correct name of this style of dwelling is "to-gun," a West African term meaning "place of assembly." The Bowmans built onto the house, adding a bedroom, dining room, and kitchen. In the back, there was a goldfish pond and a henhouse stocked with chickens.

As an only child of parents with some means, Bertha was indulged and encouraged. She played with the children on her block, rode her red tricycle up and down the street, and looked forward to rides in her red wagon. She had a beautiful playhouse in her backyard where she spent many happy hours. Bertha loved for her mother to read to her and enjoyed a wide assortment of children's books. She had a large collection of dolls and, like many young girls, spent hours hosting tea parties. Her friends would come over and enjoy sandwiches and cookies made by Mrs. Bowman. All of Bertha's dolls were white, since this was before the time of ethnic toys. She also had her beloved little white dog.

As she grew up, Bertha enjoyed the normal childhood pastimes of hopscotch and jumping rope as her plaits flew in the air. Bertha and her friends would sing the popular children's song "Little Sally Walker." Taking turns, they called out, "Little Sally Walker sittin' in a saucer, ride, Sally, ride!" Her friends were African American, since the races did not ordinarily mingle. Sometimes, however, the children of African American domestic workers might play with the children of their mothers' employers when they accompanied them to work.

Tall like her father, Bertha was always dressed nicely in clothes made by her mother. She had lots of dresses from which to choose. Mrs. Bowman was a talented seamstress and hatmaker. At that time, proper dress for a woman would include a hat. Women wore gloves in addition to hats when going to church and for special occasions or outings. Mrs. Bowman was also skilled at making wedding hats. Like other girls, Bertha wore large bows in her plaited hair.

Another of Mrs. Bowman's many talents was music. She was an accomplished pianist and organist. She passed on her love of music to her young daughter. Mrs. Bowman sang to Bertha as an infant and young Bertha grew up loving to sing. She had a beautiful voice and was not shy about using it. Bertha enjoyed learning the spirituals, and throughout her life she would use her musical talents to enrich the lives of others. She often joined the multitude of children who gathered at "Mother" Ricker's house where they were taught the spirituals and the meaning behind the songs. Through the spirituals, the children learned stories from the Bible, particularly those of hope and deliverance in the Hebrew Scriptures. Mother Ricker was just one of many elders in the community who passed down lessons to the children. They imparted the values of the community, whether it was respect, responsibility, perseverance, or some other character trait or moral. Besides nourishing their souls, Mother Ricker often fed their stomachs.

Mrs. Bowman also taught her daughter to play the piano. The family had a baby grand piano, unusual in an African American home at that time. Her mother played for

Sunday services at several local churches. Bertha frequently accompanied her and was always dressed properly in a Sunday church dress and shoes and the ever-present hair bows.

As a member of the E. W. Rogers Federated Club in Canton, Mrs. Bowman and other local women were engaged in many social and service activities. Mrs. Bowman's mother was a founder of the Mississippi State Federation of Colored Women's Clubs in 1903. The Canton club raised money for numerous causes, including community beautification projects and college scholarships for young African American high school students. The women knew the importance of education and were more than happy to undertake initiatives to help the youth in their community.

Bertha was accustomed to spending time around older adults who were contemporaries of her parents. Her parents were older than many of her friends' parents because she was born thirteen years after her parents were married. Mrs. Bowman was thirty-five at the time of her birth, while Dr. Bowman was forty-three. While the average age for giving birth in the United States has increased over the years, having children at that age was more unusual in the late 1930s. Many of her parents' friends were grandparents or even great-grandparents themselves. As a child, Bertha could not help but be influenced by them, which led many people, including Bertha herself, to describe her as an "old folk's child." As a result, not only was she comfortable in the presence of older people, but she grew up with admiration, compassion, and respect for them. She clearly recognized the hardships that so many people had endured, particularly in the South, and was inspired by their forbearance, courage, and strength.

As professionals, Bertha's parents wanted the best education for her. Unfortunately, options were limited by state-mandated segregation and Bertha would have to go to Cameron Street, the local public school. Built in 1913, after the closing of several smaller rural schools, Cameron Street was the first consolidated school for African American students in Canton. Dr. Bowman dutifully took his daughter to and from school each day, making sure that she arrived safely and on time. Bertha attended this school from first through fifth grade.

The Bowmans were not happy with the education Bertha was receiving and feared she would fall behind. The school did not have the resources that a white school would have. In the 1896 landmark case, *Plessy v. Ferguson*, the U.S. Supreme Court ruled that segregation was legal if facilities for both black and white races were equal. However, it would be difficult, if not impossible, for a poor state like Mississippi to support even *one* quality public school system, let alone two. Even today, Mississippi is below most other states in school rankings.

Bertha's parents strongly valued education and wanted better options for their daughter. Her father was a graduate of the 1918 class at Meharry Medical College in Nashville, Tennessee. Her mother was sent from her home in Greenville in Washington County in the Mississippi Delta to Tougaloo in Madison County for high school since there was not an African American high school in Greenville at the time. She received her diploma from Tougaloo Academy-Tougaloo College in May 1919. Students in communities without an African American high school had to leave their homes and families during the school term if they wished to go beyond the eighth grade. They would board with other families or live in school dormitories. Students who could not leave their homes had limited opportunities with only an eighth-grade education. Mrs. Bowman continued at Tougaloo College, where she was awarded her A.B. (bachelor's) degree from their Teacher's College in 1921.

Bertha's maternal grandmother, Lizzie W. Coleman, was an accomplished educator who served as a teacher and an elementary school principal for over forty years. She pushed her students to excel and was formidable in her own right. A strict disciplinarian, she expected students to obey the rules. As a principal, Mrs. Coleman made sure that her African American school had the resources to educate and prepare its students, despite the climate in which they lived. She was selective of the teachers that she hired and required new teachers to observe experienced ones and work under their guidance for a time. Each teacher was expected to raise $150 annually for the school, not an insignificant amount of money in the early part of the twentieth century. In today's dollars, it would be about $4,000.

While Mrs. Coleman excelled at math, her real devotion was to literature, particularly poetry. She was an avid reader, and frequently lectured on prominent African American authors, poets, and playwrights from the Harlem Renaissance (1920s–early 1930s), including Jamaican-born Claude McKay, Langston Hughes, and Countee Cullen. She was known for her ability to recite long passages or verses from memory. Mrs. Coleman's years of service and commitment to her students and community were recognized in 1920, when one of the first African American high schools was named after her—Coleman High School in Greenville, where she lived and worked as an adult. While the school opened too late for Mrs. Bowman to attend, she taught there briefly before her marriage. It is now Coleman Middle School, serving students in grades six through eight. A historic marker bears Mrs. Coleman's motto, "Burn the midnight oil! Be prepared!" Her achievements were so great that she is still honored today. Sadly, Bertha's maternal grandmother died on May 28, 1931, several years before her granddaughter was born. With the Coleman and Bowman educational backgrounds, the Bowmans were desperate to find the right school for their daughter where she could both learn and flourish.

Life in a segregated society was not easy, particularly in the Deep South of Bertha's childhood. While Dr. Bowman was held in some esteem in the African American community as a physician, that same esteem was not equally held by the white community, in which he and his medical degree would be scorned. Despite Dr. Bowman's education, his service to his country during World War I, and his calm and professional demeanor, he was treated with contempt by many in the white community, including other medical professionals. How demeaning it must have been to him to hear a pharmacist at Guy's Drug Store, which filled his prescriptions, refer to him as "Bowman" rather than with his hard-earned professional title of "doctor." This indignity was yet another example of how race impacted almost everything in Mississippi's history.

Despite professional indignities, Dr. Bowman was faithful to his chosen career path. He selected Canton as a place to practice because there was a need for medical care for the many African American residents. It had long been his desire to go into medicine to help people. He fulfilled his desire by practicing in a medically underserved area. As was common in a rural practice, Dr. Bowman accepted all forms of payments from his patients, including eggs, chickens, and freshly grown vegetables. This was the only way that some patients could pay for their medical care. He made house calls in his trusty Ford to those with and without money to pay him. His patients were grateful for his care and remembered him at Christmas with gifts. As a general practitioner, he was called on to perform a wide variety of medical procedures from pulling teeth to deliveries of hundreds of babies in their homes. He had to be prepared as he never knew what to expect from a patient who had limited access to medical care.

In 1974, on his eightieth birthday, Dr. Bowman was recognized by the Minority Education Foundation of Mississippi. At the time, he was the oldest practicing doctor in the state. Despite the obstacles and indignities that he faced during his career, Dr. Bowman persevered and practiced medicine until he was about eighty-five years old. Young Bertha grew up knowing of her father's strong commitment to his patients and to the community he served.

Chapter 2

A NEW SCHOOL IN CANTON

There were never very many Catholics in Mississippi, especially in the first half of the twentieth century. Mississippians were more likely to be Protestant, particularly Baptist. However, as a poor state and one that offered many opportunities to evangelize, leaders of religious orders in the United States frequently sent priests, sisters, and brothers to serve in Mississippi, as there were not enough native religious vocations. The Mississippi bishops welcomed outside assistance. From 1911 to 1984, there were nearly seventy women's religious orders serving in Mississippi, where the sisters ministered in the fields of education, health care, and social services. More than a thousand priests served in the state during that same time.

Efforts were made to increase the number of religious vocations when the Society of the Divine Word (SVD) established Sacred Heart Seminary for African Americans in Greenville, Mississippi, in 1920. This seminary was met with great resistance by some white residents, including members of the Ku Klux Klan. Consequently, in 1923, the order relocated the seminary to Bay St. Louis on the Gulf Coast. This area had a larger African American Catholic population and was more hospitable to Catholics. It was renamed St. Augustine Seminary after the African bishop and saint, who was a "Doctor of the Church." (This title, derived from the Latin word for "teacher," is bestowed on certain saints.) On May 23, 1934, Sacred Heart Seminary ordained the first four African American SVD candidates for the priesthood in the United States.

The Missionary Servants of the Most Holy Trinity (ST), a male religious order, came to Mississippi as missionaries in the 1940s. In 1946, Bishop Richard O. Gerow, then the bishop of Natchez, Mississippi, asked one of the order's priests, Father Andrew Lawrence, ST, to initiate evangelization efforts in the African American community in Canton. The city had a large African American population; however, more than two-thirds of the residents had no religious affiliation.

Father Lawrence sought to secure land where they might eventually build a church and related buildings, such as a convent, rectory, and school. However, it was difficult to find someone in Canton who was willing to sell property that would be used by African Americans, especially a parcel large enough to meet future needs. After several months of searching, Father Lawrence was finally able to purchase three and a half acres from a Catholic bank president in the only large, undeveloped area, located in the African American part of Canton known as Frog Hollow. Far from ideal, the property was considered useless swampland. The purchased parcel of land bore an appropriate name, as it was inhabited by frogs, mosquitoes, and land crabs. If that did not pose enough problems, the property was near railroad yards and a fertilizer plant. With all these obstacles, it is no wonder that the land had remained vacant and undeveloped. The one structure on the property, a "small bungalow," initially served as a temporary convent for the sisters and later as a rectory for the priests.

After purchasing the land, the next task was to build a convent that could house four sisters. Three sisters of the Missionary Servants of the Blessed Trinity worked with the priests in their evangelization efforts in the community. The formal opening of the Holy Child Jesus Mission took place on September 8, 1946. For that occasion, twelve men erected on the property a large mission cross that was cut from trees contributed by the family of one of the few local African American Catholics. The cross was blessed by the mission's first pastor, Father Justin Furman, ST, a recently ordained priest.

The priests obtained two wood-frame former Army barracks, which they disassembled for transport. They were then reassembled, painted, and furnished on the mission property. The barracks were meant to be temporary, until they could build more permanent structures. One of the barracks, used for a small chapel so that Mass could be celebrated, also housed a clinic and a kindergarten. The second barrack was converted into a combined first- and second-grade classroom. By the close of the 1947–48 school year, the mission had enrolled sixty children in these early grades. They also sponsored a Girl Scout troop.

As people in the community became aware of the mission and its efforts, attendance at Mass in the chapel grew. Only a handful of the people were Catholic, but those who gathered were a devoted and loyal group. Some of the worshippers expressed their devotion by calling out "Amen" during Mass. One local resident who was actively involved in the mission's efforts was Mrs. Bowman, who lived a short distance away. She could always be counted on to play the organ when asked. Bertha frequently joined her mother. She enjoyed singing at Mass with a group of other girls, and soon became their leader.

By the late summer of 1947, Father Furman was reassigned and succeeded by the second pastor, Father Gilbert Hay, ST. As part of the early outreach efforts, the priests and sisters of Holy Child Jesus Mission had been visiting families in their homes and meeting with local African American residents to discuss their needs and concerns. They continued to pursue these efforts. Many of the residents believed that the public school system in Canton offered their children an inferior education. They identified improving educational opportunities as a primary need in the community. This need tied in with a major principle of the founder of the Missionary Servants of the Most Holy Trinity, Father Thomas Augustine Judge, CM: "Save the child and you save all."

The sisters working in Canton engaged in missionary work, operated the clinic, and taught the children enrolled in the early grades, but their order was not dedicated to teaching and could not staff the school long term. If a school was to be established, the pastor knew they needed to find a teaching order of sisters. Father Hay began searching for such a religious order. He knew of the Franciscan Sisters of Perpetual Adoration (FSPA), as they had a history of supporting missionary work and had supported him in the past. The order had a special group that sent money and clothing to home missions with funds raised from Catholic school children, donations, and the sale of canceled stamps to collectors.

In need of teaching sisters for several mission schools in the South, Father Lawrence met with some members of the FSPA when visiting their home state of Wisconsin. The

FSPA has German roots and is headquartered in La Crosse. Although initially founded in the United States to teach children of German immigrants, its members were known to respond to other situations where there was need. Between Father Lawrence and Father Hay, and a visit to Canton by the superior of the order, the priests were able to convince the FSPA of their urgent need for sisters. Knowing some of the hardships that the African American people in Canton faced, the order was happy to support the priests' efforts.

In the summer of 1948, four sisters, including a musician and a nurse, arrived to staff the new school, known as Holy Child Jesus. Three of the sisters would teach, while the nurse would operate the clinic and perform housekeeping duties. By the start of the 1948–49 school year, ninety-five students were registered, most of whom were not Catholic. They came from many Protestant traditions. Some were the children of ministers and leaders in their respective churches, while others had no church affiliation. The families were all attracted to the new school for one reason—the possibility of a better education and future for their children.

When she was ten, Bertha Bowman's parents withdrew her from her public school and enrolled her in the sixth grade at Holy Child Jesus School. Her parents, like others in the community, now had a better option for their daughter. Like many of her classmates, Bertha was behind grade level as she started the new school year. In fact, many new students were so far behind that they were classified as "ungraded." Reading was a problem for Bertha and the others. All the new students were reading below the second-grade level.

Because of limited resources, the school was stocked with many donated items, including books, clothes, and supplies. Donations were solicited from around the country. Families who could afford it were asked to pay a monthly tuition of two dollars. The school also encouraged parents to volunteer, and Mrs. Bowman could always be counted on to help. Mrs. Bowman's willingness to serve where needed would leave a lasting impression on her young daughter. Bertha learned at an early age from both her parents the importance of giving back to your community.

Father Hay knew that the school needed a permanent structure in order to grow, as they were still limited in the number of students they could accept and grades they could offer. He wanted a brick building because he knew from experience how much damage termites did to wooden structures in the South. He had a small brick school built, housing four classrooms, and designed for adding more classrooms later. The new school was dedicated by Bishop Gerow on September 20, 1949. A year after the school was built, two more classrooms were added, which now provided space for 150 students. When Father Hay was reassigned after serving for four years, Father Furman returned as the third pastor in late March 1951.

In the fall of that year, the school space was increased once again by adding two large classrooms to the structure. In addition, they were able to provide indoor plumbing, a luxury they, like many other rural African American schools and homes, did not have. Besides indoor restrooms, the additions brought a teacher's lounge and a music room.

Teachers from the FSPA opened a new world to the students at Holy Child Jesus School. The traditional classes taught during the day brought Bertha and many of the other students up to grade level. Bertha spent many hours reading about Dick and Jane and completing exercises in the widely used *Think-and-Do Book*. As she rapidly advanced in reading, she completed the grade levels of the series in one school year. She used her newly acquired skills to help other students read while they helped her in math.

The sisters also offered additional activities after the school day and over the weekend. For most of the students, this was their first time interacting daily with non-African Americans. While the opening of the school addressed one pressing issue, there were many more needs in the community. The sisters sought to address some of these needs by offering classes for adults on different health topics and a Wednesday well-baby clinic, which was popular among young mothers.

The sisters also opened a used clothing store stocked with donated items sent from other parts of the country. The sisters' resourcefulness was unmatched in obtaining what they needed. They did a great amount of local fundraising, including the popular annual community-wide bazaar, and the students and families participated in their efforts. The students knew they were helping the school and themselves.

Fortunately, having a sister with musical talent on staff enabled the school and mission to offer both a student and an adult choir. Bertha happily joined the school choir. Mrs. Bowman provided musical accompaniment on many occasions.

The students at Holy Child Jesus School experienced and deeply felt the love and dedication of the FSPA sisters. They not only learned from them, but they were inspired by their commitment to the community. The sisters did not just teach the corporal works of mercy that Jesus taught (Matt 25), but they lived them as well. They followed the spirit of St. Francis of Assisi, who abandoned his life with its privileges of nobility and trappings of wealth to live the gospel in simplicity, while tending to those in need and caring for all of God's creation. The sisters were extraordinary models of faith. How could their students not be inspired by their tireless dedication?

While the sisters were a source of inspiration to many of their students, there was at least one among them who was more than inspired. As a teenager, Bertha Bowman aspired to become a sister, too. At this time in the Church's history in the United States, many young Catholics felt called to serve God and the Church. It was not uncommon to have two or more children from the same family serving as a priest, sister, or brother. Many reasons led a young person to a religious vocation. Sometimes it was the influence of their mother or their Catholic school. Other times it was knowing a sister, brother, or priest. But Bertha was different from most. At the age of fifteen and a half, she aspired to join the order that she had come to know at her school, which was not in itself unusual. However, the sisters were from a white religious order with German roots. Their motherhouse, or headquarters, was in Wisconsin, a long way in both distance and culture from her home in Canton, Mississippi, but this did not discourage Bertha. She was determined to go to Wisconsin despite her parents' fierce objections.

Bertha would always remember the impact that the first FSPA sisters in Canton had on her. She later expressed gratitude for everything these sisters had offered her and the other students. They taught the children that they could have a future and that regardless of one's background or race, people could live and work together. Coming from a small, segregated community in the South, these were ideals that may not have been possible without the vision that the sisters instilled in their students. The children of Holy Child Jesus School could have dreams just like any other child, and, with hard work and perseverance, they could see them realized.

Bertha's calling to become a sister was not something that Dr. and Mrs. Bowman could have anticipated. Bertha was not a cradle Catholic, nor were her parents. Her mother was Episcopalian and her father was Methodist. Bertha converted to Catholicism in June 1947, after being inspired by the Catholic missionary sisters and priests she had met in Canton and by the Church's commitment to social justice. Already at the age of nine, she could see the good works being performed by the Church and its ministers. Bertha was baptized as an infant on February 13, 1938, at St. Mark's Episcopal Church in Jackson, Mississippi, in her mother's tradition. During her early years, Bertha accompanied her mother to church on Sundays. Later on—in fact, years after Bertha's conversion to Catholicism—both her parents converted as well, her mother first.

The Bowmans tried unsuccessfully to dissuade their headstrong teenager from leaving home and the only life she knew. They even enlisted the pastor of Holy Child Jesus Mission in their efforts. Both he and her parents tried to convince Bertha that if she was truly called to be a sister, then she should join the Sisters of the Holy Family in New Orleans, an African American order, which was founded in 1842. As an only child, she would be closer to home and in a more familiar environment. The Bowman's fears of sending their protected daughter so far away were based on the world in which they lived. And what about grandchildren? Were they destined to have none from their only child?

Bertha's family worried about how a young African American teenager would fare by herself in a place far from her home and culture. After all, she was only fifteen and a half. She had not even graduated from high school. And a white religious order? Bertha was raised in a segregated African

American community with its own culture and expectations. How would she adapt?

No amount of debate or threats would dissuade Bertha. She was going to join the Franciscan Sisters of Perpetual Adoration and would travel to their motherhouse in Wisconsin. So that she would not travel alone, an FSPA sister accompanied Bertha on the train as she began her journey.

Because Jim Crow laws were still in effect and they traveled by train, Bertha and the sister would not ordinarily be permitted to sit together. The name Jim Crow comes from a black slave portrayed in the nineteenth century by a white actor, Thomas D. Rice, who mocked African Americans in his song and dance routine. The name came to be associated with the laws and customs that enforced segregation in the South. There were several Jim Crow railroad laws in Mississippi. Railcars traveling to and from the South were segregated. In addition, a train station had segregated waiting rooms, ticket windows, and restrooms. Bertha and the sister may have packed food, since she could not have eaten in the dining car. While both the railroad company and the conductor could be fined for violating the law, somehow arrangements were made for Bertha and the sister to travel together.

Whether Bertha's self-confidence and courage came from her mother or father is debatable. What is not is that she was an intelligent, independent, passionate, and fiercely determined young woman, and there was nothing that would stand in her way. At fifteen and a half, Bertha knew what she wanted and what she believed God was calling her to do. She bade farewell to the life she knew and looked forward to where her journey would take her.

Chapter 3

A RELIGIOUS VOCATION

After the long train ride, including a two-day layover in Chicago, where Bertha and her traveling companion stayed at a convent, they finally arrived in La Crosse, located in the western part of Wisconsin along the Mississippi River. The order moved from Jefferson, Wisconsin, in 1871, when the Diocese of La Crosse was formed.

In 1953, as a teenager, Bertha needed to make many adjustments as she entered St. Rose of Viterbo Convent. It was a large complex and the convent consisted of five floors, with 183 residents, including professed sisters and those in different stages of formation. There were also three chapels, one of which was the adoration chapel. This chapel was especially important for the order, whose name became the Franciscan Sisters of Perpetual Adoration in 1878. Since the late nineteenth century, members of the community have continuously taken turns to pray before the Blessed Sacrament day and night in this chapel.

Bertha was assigned to a dormitory in the convent. Known as a "cell," she had a designated space furnished with the necessities of a bed, chair, and dresser. The white curtains separating the cells were closed in the evening for privacy. Bertha traded her traveling clothes for a plain black dress that she had brought with her. In a formal ceremony, she was given a black veil to wear in the chapel.

As the only African American in her religious community, Bertha needed to adapt to being in the minority. She had been in the majority in Canton, where there was little interaction or relationship with the white community. Bertha, known initially as an aspirant (one who "aspires" to join religious life), learned to live in community with the other aspirants regardless of their backgrounds. It was a time of adjustment for all of them. Just as her parents feared, she also had to adjust to the comments and behaviors of some of the sisters, not all of whom were as kind or as accepting of her as those she knew in Canton. Bertha, however, was eager to please and to succeed in her formation, so she tried her best to blend in with the other aspirants, no matter how difficult or trying that was to do. Because she knew how to be circumspect around whites as a child in her segregated hometown, she would employ those same tactics now as she navigated the formation process. Just as she discovered at Holy Child Jesus School, there were sisters at St. Rose who welcomed and guided her along the way.

Besides living with people of different racial, cultural, and geographic backgrounds, Bertha had to adapt to very different cultural traditions. The food at the convent was quite different from what she was used to in the South. Instead of the favored collard greens, okra, catfish, fried chicken, sweet potato pie, and sweet tea of home, she was introduced to heartier German-style food, including kielbasa (Polish sausage), other meats, and potatoes. Wisconsin was also known for its cheese. Many of the early German settlers brought their own customs and foods to their new homeland, not unlike African slaves who brought traditional foods with them, such as the southern tradition of black-eyed peas and okra.

Mealtimes at St. Rose were different for Bertha as well. Rather than talking about her day with her parents in her normal energetic manner, two of the three daily meals at the convent were eaten in silence, while a member of the community read from books on spirituality, and on St. Francis and other saints. Lunch was the only meal where Bertha and the others could converse.

And the weather! Bertha had to become accustomed to the freezing temperatures of winter in the northern Midwest, so unlike the more temperate winters at home. She exchanged the sweltering months of heat and humidity in Mississippi for months of snow and ice in Wisconsin throughout the long and cold winters. Bertha did not need to worry about getting exercise during the frequent snowstorms—one of the tasks assigned to aspirants was clearing snow from the sidewalks. She learned to wear multiple layers of clothes to stay warm.

Bertha's days were soon established with a regular routine. Her schedule included Mass, school, community work, activities in the convent and chapel, and prayer. She and the others engaged in outdoor activities together by roller skating, playing softball, or just walking and enjoying nature. Inside, they played cards and some board games. Bertha enjoyed her classes at St. Rose High School. She did very well academically and seemed to be happily adjusting to her new life. She joyfully sang in the St. Rose choir. Bertha also kept in contact with her family through her many letters. Thankfully for her parents (and for her), she was able to travel home for about ten days during her first Christmas at St. Rose.

Religious life follows a prescribed path of formation or preparation in the years before final vows are taken in a community. The formation is important as it allows for the person to consider whether she is truly called to religious life and for the religious order to discern whether the person is meant to be a member of that community. After her time as an aspirant, Bertha began a period called postulancy. In the FSPA community, this period begins on February 2, the Feast of the Presentation of the Lord, when Jesus's parents took him to the temple in Jerusalem. She and the others were given new clothes to wear, including a black dress with a detachable white collar and a black veil, which she would now always wear in public. The clothes symbolized a change in their identity; each step in the formation process was signified by a change in the garments that they wore. During this period, the postulants would learn about the Rule and Constitutions of the FSPA order and discern their calling to a religious vocation.

Bertha finished her high school course work in January 1955. She began taking college classes at the order's nearby Viterbo College (now Viterbo University), a Catholic, Franciscan institution founded in 1890. She would later receive her high school diploma in May 1955.

Unfortunately, Bertha was soon diagnosed with tuberculosis (TB), a serious and highly contagious lung disease. In the first decades of the twentieth century, TB was a major cause of death throughout the world. At first, Bertha was hospitalized locally at St. Francis Hospital. After about three months, she was transferred to the River Pines Sanatorium in Stevens Point, Wisconsin. (Sanatoriums were for people who had long-term medical issues, especially TB at that time.) Mrs. Bowman came by train to accompany her daughter in the ambulance. Bertha remained at the sanatorium to rest and recuperate for the next nine and a half months. During her stay, her parents traveled to visit her. Bertha celebrated her eighteenth birthday at River Pines with a surprise visit from her mother. Her classmates regularly communicated with her, keeping her informed of any news. Her effervescent personality, even while ill, enabled her to easily make friends among the residents. She tried to keep up with some studies by taking a correspondence course through the University of Wisconsin. Her illness, though, prevented her from joining her classmates for high school graduation or from receiving her diploma in person.

Some postulants might have reconsidered their plans for a religious life, and an order might have determined that a serious illness posed too many hindrances for continuing in formation. But Bertha had Sister Charlotte Bonneville, FSPA, as her mentor and the sister to whom she reported, to advocate for her to continue pursuing her vocation. Because of Bertha's illness and long convalescence, she was a year behind. However, the order changed the formation program at that time, reducing the number of years from six to five, beginning with Bertha's class of 1958. The change enabled Bertha to remain on schedule and continue with her same class.

The next stage in the formation process is known as the novitiate, when a postulant is formally received into a religious community. This stage of instruction and study is more challenging. Bertha and the other novices were now addressed as sisters. As was the custom, on August 12, 1956, Bertha was given a religious name: Sister Mary Thea. Thea, meaning "of God," was the name of an early fourth-century martyr who was killed alongside her friend Valentina. It also closely approximates her father's name, Theon, of Greek derivation and meaning "godly." Sister Thea had never been fond of her birth name and was happy to receive her new religious name.

As a novice, Sister Thea's change of clothing once again reflected her stage in the formation process. She was given a long black habit, the distinct clothing worn by her order at that time, a white collar, and a white cap for her hair, which was covered by a white veil. Only her hands and face were uncovered. She also wore a white cincture, or robe belt, around her waist that was tied three times, representing the three vows that she and the other novices would take: poverty, chastity, and obedience.

The two-year novitiate included instruction in different aspects of religious life. The novices would study the significance of the vows or promises that they would later make. The vows are a significant commitment and it is important that novices understand the life choices that they are making. Also, they would continue to learn about the Rule or Constitutions that guide their order and, as a Franciscan community, they would learn more about the lives of St. Francis and of St. Clare of Assisi. St. Clare chose to leave her wealthy family, similarly to St. Francis's story, so she too could follow Jesus. The novices would learn different types of prayer, including meditation where they would quietly reflect on scripture, perhaps a word, verse, or image. As before, they were assigned household tasks. The novices were now more restricted in their outside contact, including access to family (they could only write one letter a month home), radio, and newspapers. In the second year of the novitiate, Sister Thea and other sisters who planned to teach studied at Viterbo College. Sister Thea would continue there a second year to take some of the classes that she missed when she was ill.

At the end of the novitiate, on August 12, 1958, Sister Thea made her first, or "simple," vows with nineteen other sisters from her formation class. These vows were renewed in August 1959 and August 1960, providing opportunity for the novices to consider the commitment they were undertaking. Sister Thea was now twenty years old. Her parents traveled from Canton to celebrate this joyous occasion with her. As a professed sister, Thea was given a black veil to replace the white one she had received when she entered the novitiate. Each sister also received a gold ring with the letters IHS, which are the first three letters of the Holy Name of Jesus in Greek.

In the 1950s and 1960s, when many Catholic children attended parish elementary schools, there was an immense need for teachers on an ongoing basis. The need was so great that members of religious communities were often assigned to teach before they graduated from college or received any type of teacher certification. Sometimes sisters would have to attend college part time or in the summer so they would be available to teach in their schools.

As was their practice, in the summer of 1959, the FSPA sisters were informed by "mission slips" where they would be assigned or "missioned" for the coming year. Sister Thea was sent to Blessed Sacrament, an affluent parish school in La Crosse. She would be the only African American among the teaching staff and students. At that time, the racial composition of the city was overwhelmingly white. Although La Crosse was a northern city, African Americans were strongly dissuaded from making the city their home. La Crosse has been described as one of the nation's many "sundown towns" or cities, where town leaders embraced segregated practices that restricted nonwhites from living there. According to the population census of 1960, only 21 of the 45,747 people living in the city of La Crosse were identified as black.

While some parents at Blessed Sacrament School were initially alarmed about Sister Thea's placement, neither her order nor the school, whose principal was an FSPA sister, were willing to change her assignment. True to form, Sister Thea won over her fifth- and sixth-grade students and their families with her sparkling personality and her natural skills and talents. She found herself at home in the classroom, and discovered it was a place she could shine. Sister Thea radiated joy. Although she was only twenty-one and did not have teaching experience, she soon developed a rapport with the families of students. To the delight of many of them, she was appointed to teach the same grades at the school the following year.

After two years at Blessed Sacrament, Sister Thea was about to receive a new assignment that would bring great joy to her parents. Her new mission was to Holy Child Jesus School in Canton. She had hoped that one day she would be able to teach there, in her hometown, close to her parents. She was about to come full circle, being able to teach and touch the lives of so many children just as she had been by the first sisters in her order. After eight years of being away from home, at the age of twenty-three, Sister Thea was finally returning. She took summer classes at Viterbo College and then returned by train to Canton.

Sister Thea taught at Holy Child Jesus School from August 1961 to August 1968. She enjoyed her time as a teacher there. Once again, her love of teaching and of her students endeared her to many. She passed on numerous lessons to others over the years.

Because of her natural ability to teach, Sister Thea felt strongly that there are many ways to reach children. There was no set formula that could be used for every student. During Sister Thea's time at Holy Child Jesus School, she taught elementary and high school classes. She found that some of the older students were not as interested in learning as she had been. While she may have found this disappointing, Sister Thea devised a way to engage uncooperative or even defiant students. She recognized that many of the students did not have the same opportunities as those she had taught at Blessed Sacrament in La Crosse. Still, she was committed to creating an environment that was conducive to her students' learning.

Because Sister Thea had a lifelong love of music, she chose to incorporate it into her classroom. She was a strong believer that learning could be fun. Through poetry, music, and other art forms involving movement, such as dance and drama, her classroom burst with the exuberance for which she was known.

The fifty-student choir that Sister Thea directed was rewarded for their hard work, perseverance, and talent, with the production of the album *The Voice of Negro America* in 1967. The album comprised fourteen spirituals. How proud the students, their families, the school community, and Sister Thea must have been!

Sister Thea expressed her cultural identity through music and dance, and she inspired her students to do so as well. Her students loved being active by giving performances, and Sister Thea loved watching them participate and shine. As she would later say, "Jesus gave it to me, I'm gonna let it shine," from one of her favorite songs, "This Little Light of Mine." She passed on that joy-filled spirit to her students. She brought a spirit to the classroom that was clearly contagious.

To overcome obstacles facing some children, Sister Thea believed that it was important for schools to provide a conducive environment for students to learn and thrive. As she said, "Our children are longing to be loved. They have to know they are somebody. We have to create within our schools an environment in which every child is special." She decorated the walls in her classroom with pictures of black biblical figures and African saints so that her students could not only learn about them but be reminded of the contributions of holy people of color. Sister Thea knew how important it was for children to have confidence in themselves and believe in their abilities. She wanted schools and parents to convey the message, "You're somebody special 'cause you're God's child."

Sister Thea also believed that students could learn from each other and not just from teachers. She had older students help younger ones, and those who excelled in a subject, regardless of age, would help someone else who might not be as proficient, just as she had helped others as a sixth grader. By helping each other, everyone would benefit. As a child, she was taught by the elders in her community the African proverb "Each one teach one," and she brought this maxim into the classroom. She knew that this teaching style would help students more than the white competitive model that most schools used. Given the right opportunities, Sister Thea believed that all children and youth, regardless of their circumstances, could succeed. Just as each of us are called to share our God-given gifts and talents with others to build up the Body of Christ, the Church, Sister Thea learned from her African American community to "Pass it on! Share it! Share the gifts! Share the wealth!"

During the school year, Sister Thea lived at the Holy Child Jesus convent with the other FSPA sisters. However, her living arrangements were controversial among some in Canton's white community. Because the other sisters were white, they preferred that the convent remain segregated. For safety reasons, Sister Thea could not travel by car with the FSPA sisters and would have to be driven by her parents to meet the sisters at their destination. When she did risk being in the same car, she would duck if a car with white passengers or the police passed by—certainly not easy because of her height and expansive religious habit!

On August 10, 1963, in the order's magnificent Mary of the Angels Chapel, Sister Thea professed her final or perpetual vows as an FSPA sister with fifty-four sisters from the two combined formation classes. She was now a fully professed member of the community. She received a silver medal of the congregation, a Maltese cross with eight points, representing the Beatitudes or teachings from Jesus's Sermon on the Mount. Her parents traveled to La Crosse to attend this momentous occasion. Sister Thea then returned to Canton to prepare for the new school year.

Each summer during the years that Sister Thea taught in Canton, she returned to La Crosse to continue studying for her undergraduate degree at Viterbo College. She was majoring in English with a minor in speech and drama. After ten years of study, Sister Thea received her bachelor's degree in July 1965, graduating *magna cum laude*.

In June 1966, she continued her practice of studying in the summer. She left Canton to begin part-time graduate study at The Catholic University of America (CUA) in Washington, D.C., to study English literature. It appeared that Sister Thea was following in the footsteps of her maternal grandmother in her love of poetry and literature. As a summer student, Sister Thea joined other Washington-based FSPA sisters who were living in a convent of a French-Canadian order. She was ready to begin her graduate studies.

Chapter 4

UPHEAVAL IN THE SOUTH

For Americans who did not grow up in the American South of the 1940s, 1950s, and even 1960s, it is hard to imagine what life was like for African Americans, particularly for those in rural or smaller communities like Canton. Life was hard, good paying jobs were scarce, especially those that did not involve agriculture, and there always seemed to be trouble to avoid.

Many of the opportunities that are taken for granted now, such as where to live, what school or place of worship to attend, who to vote for, or even what restaurant to patronize were not necessarily options for African Americans. There were many restrictions due to segregation. African Americans had to use separate water fountains or a dipper or cup if there was only one fountain. Also, instead of two restrooms, one for women and one for men, there might be three so that one could be used solely by African Americans, regardless of gender.

In an interview for a local television show, following her keynote address in Milwaukee for a twentieth-anniversary commemoration of the assassination of Dr. Martin Luther

King Jr., Sister Thea spoke of the indignities she experienced in having to use a water fountain with a broken bowl when cold water was available in the fountain for whites. She also recalled all the times her family was traveling and there were no restrooms available for African Americans. Travel was particularly difficult for the Bowmans and other African Americans, as they had to find places to stay, and gas stations and restaurants that would serve them. African American travelers would often have no other alternative than to rent a room in a private home. As Sister Thea and so many others routinely experienced, life was unjust and not equal; there seemed to be no way around it.

For Sister Thea and her family, segregation was an everyday part of life. She and other children learned early how to navigate their way so as not to provoke trouble. They were taught what they could or could not do, or they learned by example. What African American children were taught was vastly different than what their white counterparts were taught. During the interview, Sister Thea remembered how insulting it was for her middle-aged mother to be called by her first name by a young store clerk, while a white teenager was referred to by the proper title of "Miss." This lack of respect was the same indignity that her father, a doctor, experienced as well. Shopping in a store could also present problems, as Sister Thea recalled. She had to wait until all the white customers had been served before she could be helped. These "etiquette norms" under Jim Crow, while humiliating, had to be followed. There was no recourse.

While inequalities were everywhere, one just had to make do. For those who did not behave as expected, the consequences were often swift and unjust. African American parents did not want to expose their children to the consequences, which could be quite dire, and tried to steer their children in a different direction to avoid backlash. They walked a fine line between encouraging their children's independence and curiosity and protecting them from the harsh realities of their life. As a child, Sister Thea once drank from a whites-only water fountain. Her mother's fast response ensured there would be no second try.

Considering the hardships that African Americans in the South faced, why did they just not leave their homes and go someplace where they might encounter fewer restrictions and more opportunities? Many African Americans did leave the South in the Great Migration (1916–70). Six million African Americans left during those years in search of freedom and jobs. They headed first to northern cities such as Chicago, Detroit, and New York. Later, they traveled further west to Oakland and Los Angeles in California, and elsewhere.

However, not everyone could just pick up and move. People frequently had generational ties to their communities and were unable or unwilling to leave their families or homes for a distant and unknown place. Others could not afford to move or were too old or too ill to embark upon a new life. Fannie Lou Hamer, the Mississippi civil rights activist and organizer, pointed out still another problem in relocating: "Why should I leave Ruleville, and why should I leave Mississippi? I go to the big city and with the kind of education they give us in Mississippi, I got problems. I'd wind up in a soup line there. That's why I want to change Mississippi. You don't run away from problems; you just face them."

How would there ever be change if everybody left? Was life better for an African American outside the South? Many of those who chose to leave found to their dismay that life in the North and in the West wasn't the panacea they hoped it would be. They might not have to pick cotton and other crops, and there were no official Jim Crow laws, but there was still segregation and discrimination in many areas.

Rather than uprooting themselves and their families, some African Americans tried to make subtle changes in their communities while others just tried to live quiet and meaningful lives, remaining vigilant of their surroundings. The Bowman family chose to stay in the South and make a life for themselves, and to make life better for others.

As the Bowmans had experienced, a quality education was a problem unless there were alternatives. In 1954, in *Brown v. Education*, the U.S. Supreme Court ruled against segregation in public schools and outlawed the "separate but equal" rule. Segregation continued to exist in many places, however, including in Mississippi. Also, as a result of *Brown v. Education*, a new form of segregation arose with the opening of private white academies, including Canton Academy in Sister Thea's hometown. These schools grew significantly in numbers in the late 1960s to early 1970s leading to a white exodus from the public school system in many places.

Church worship was another problem for the African American Catholic residents of Canton. The city already had a long-established white Catholic Church, Sacred Heart, located in the white part of town. The church had long ties to the community, as the original church was built in 1860, while the present church was dedicated in 1929. But where could black Catholics worship if they were not welcome at Sacred Heart? Would they be relegated to a designated area in a white church, such as a back pew as the early African American Catholics in Canton were, or to a balcony as in other churches?

The Holy Child Jesus Mission was founded before there was a church. The school opened first because of the immediate need for better quality education. Schools were also an important way to evangelize. Canton did not originally have enough African American Catholics to support a church; it would take time for people to become familiar with the Catholic Church and its rituals. As time went on, the small chapel in the old Army barracks could no longer seat all the worshippers who came to Mass, and other liturgies. In fact, the chapel could only hold fifty worshippers, far fewer than those who attended Sunday Mass.

As the community grew, church leaders knew it was time to think about building a church. In 1954, the mission community determined it was ready to have its own church. That idea brought strong resistance from town leaders and some residents, including those white residents who lived near the property. To quell the dissension, the bishop advised waiting. However, as the city continually stalled in granting approval, the money that was designated for the new church was redirected to build a brick gymnasium-auditorium for worship and other activities. The new structure would also be shared with the school. The barracks were always intended to be temporary, and, after long-term use, were not only too small but also had become structurally unsound and dangerous.

City officials made it clear that they did not want to see African Americans when they were worshipping on Sundays. While the mission already had the land to build a church on the Frog Hollow property, they still needed permits, which they were having trouble obtaining. With endless runarounds from the city, on Saturday, May 22, 1965, in a letter to the pastor of Sacred Heart to be read at the next day's Sunday Masses, Bishop Gerow requested that the pastor and parishioners of Sacred Heart Church welcome the parishioners from Holy Child Jesus Mission. The bishop firmly stated, "Since a Catholic Church is the House of God, [African American] Catholics are welcome in any of our churches." The following day, the pastor, Father Luke Mikschl, ST, led one hundred parishioners and nine sisters, including Sister Thea, from Holy Child Jesus to Sacred Heart Church. The marchers waited for the conclusion of Sacred Heart's Mass, and then celebrated their own liturgy.

In another effort to quash the building of the church, city officials would not allow the entrance of the church to face the street. In fact, they wanted the church to face the fertilizer plant. To try to address the city's concerns, Father Mikschl had fencing and landscaping added to try to obscure the property at great cost. City officials also wanted the church to be built 195 feet back from the street. Requiring the church to face away from the street was in such a stark contrast to all the majestic churches whose front steps welcomed people to pray and worship, and was intended as yet another means of degradation. After much acrimony over a period of twenty years, and numerous concessions, the parishioners of Holy Child Jesus were finally able to have their own church. The new Holy Child Jesus Church was dedicated by Bishop Gerow on April 7, 1966.

The struggle for a church was part of the larger struggle that African Americans in the South faced. This period marked a time in American history of violence, beatings, and lynchings. The Ku Klux Klan was particularly active in Mississippi. They and other white supremacists, including the Citizens' Councils, posed a significant danger to those who challenged their beliefs or tried to upset the status quo. African Americans contended with a long list of indignities and sheer hatred. Besides inferior schools, inadequate or absent medical facilities, and segregated churches and cemeteries, segregation also pertained to places for socializing, such as restaurants, theaters, parks, and swimming pools. Even some southern court houses were known to have segregated Bibles for those taking an oath. Discrimination was rampant, and to challenge it was to invoke probable violence.

While Sister Thea left her home in Mississippi in the summer of 1953, she had spent her formative years in the South, and was very much a product of it. Two summers after Sister Thea's departure, a tragic and pivotal event occurred about eighty-five miles north of Canton in the small town of Money, Mississippi. In August 1955, a fourteen-year-old African American youth visiting from Chicago, Emmett Till, was accused by the white cashier of a local grocery store of vague accusations related to his conduct. Retaliation for his alleged actions was swift, as Emmett was abducted a few days later by the store's owners, the woman's husband and his half-brother. Emmett was beaten, shot, and viciously murdered. The two men were arrested and tried by an all-male white jury, which deliberated for just over an hour before finding them not guilty. This horrific crime brought national, as well as international, attention to Mississippi. A few months after the verdict was rendered, the two men confessed to the crime, but they could not be retried. Decades later, the woman recanted her story. The event still elicits passion, as memorial markers have been repeatedly vandalized. Through legislation signed by President Barack Obama in December 2016, the Emmett Till Unsolved Civil Rights Crimes Reauthorization Act of 2016 (broadening the original legislation signed by President George W. Bush in October 2008), unsolved civil rights cases that resulted in a death that occurred before 1980 may be investigated and prosecuted. In 2018, the U.S. Department of Justice reopened the unsolved murder case of Emmett Till after receiving new information.

When Sister Thea returned to Mississippi to teach in the 1960s, she faced the realities of African American life when, for example, she could not travel in the same car as the other sisters. Car travel was very problematic. African American domestic workers had to sit in the back seat of a car if their white employers drove them home. Also, white drivers had the right-of-way at any intersection. In an interview for her order's publication in May 1988, Sister Thea said that she was profoundly influenced by growing up in Mississippi, "where so many of the struggles of life almost capsulated you."

As a multigenerational daughter of the South, Sister Thea's familial ties were bound with southern history. On her father's side she was the great-granddaughter of slaves. Her paternal great-grandparents were owned by a Mississippi family with the surname of Bowman. Their son, Sister Thea's beloved grandfather, Edward, was born in 1874, several years after the Emancipation Proclamation (January 1, 1863), although slavery lingered until it eventually ended. Mississippi did not actually ratify the Thirteenth Amendment, which abolished slavery, until 1995. However, the state neglected to file the required paperwork with the U.S. archivist, and thus the ratification was not official. An inquisitive new citizen, an immigrant, was motivated to research the topic after watching the 2012 movie *Lincoln*. He discovered the state's oversight and with the help of a colleague, notified the state. Once the correct paperwork was submitted, the amendment was officially ratified on February 7, 2013, making Mississippi the last state to do so, following Kentucky, which ratified the amendment on March 18, 1976.

While Sister Thea's time at Holy Child Jesus School from August 1961 to August 1968 coincided with some of the important civil rights actions of the 1960s, she was out of the state for other events that occurred. She was kept abreast of these events by her family and by the national news. Canton, the county seat of Madison County, named for James Madison, the fourth president of the United States, was often a hotbed of dissent.

Father Mikschl, who was appointed the fifth pastor of Holy Child Jesus in 1960 and served until 1979, was willing to challenge the status quo to fight for his parishioners and the rights he believed they deserved. He was led to speak publicly, write letters to local newspapers, participate in protests, and offer hospitality to protestors. These actions invariably angered some white residents and city leaders and placed the pastor in harm's way. Despite the concessions that he made in the location and frontage of Holy Child Jesus Church, his advocacy for African Americans did not endear him to everyone in Canton. He was considered too sympathetic to those who supported civil rights, which subjected him to scorn.

As Father Mikschl knew, there was much to fight for to secure rights for African Americans. Voter registration evoked terrible turmoil in the South, especially in Mississippi. The state erected enormous roadblocks that had to be overcome. These included residency requirements, poll taxes, and literacy tests on the Mississippi Constitution, which applicants would be expected to read and interpret. The registrar could ask an applicant any number of obscure questions of the registrar's own choosing. Even if a person memorized all 285 sections of the Constitution and answered the questions correctly, they could be told that they failed. Residents who were illiterate faced an even greater roadblock. Illiteracy was a significant issue in a state where education was so deficient and, for many, so limited through no fault of their own. Many of these residents wanted to vote as well. Countless people lost their jobs and homes, were hurt, incarcerated, and even killed just for seeking a right that other Americans could take for granted. It took tremendous courage among those brave enough to even try to fight the injustices.

More adverse attention was directed to the state of Mississippi and its penchant for racial violence with the assassination of Medgar Evers on June 29, 1963, in Jackson. Evers, the field secretary for the National Association for the Advancement of Colored People (NAACP) in Mississippi, was killed in the driveway of his home just a few hours after President John F. Kennedy had delivered a televised speech on civil rights to the nation. Following his funeral, Evers's body was taken to Washington, D.C., where twenty-five thousand people attended a public viewing at a local church before the World War II veteran was laid to rest at Arlington National Cemetery. Two months later, on August 28, 1963, a quarter of a million people gathered in Washington, D.C., one hundred years after the Emancipation Proclamation, for the historic March on Washington. They marched for jobs and freedom for African Americans, and heard Dr. Martin Luther King Jr. give his poignant "I Have a Dream" speech.

A year later, in 1964, the struggle continued during one of the most turbulent times in Mississippi's history during Freedom Summer. Nearly a thousand college students, most of whom were white, converged on the state from across the country to set up schools and other community efforts for both African American adults and children. Many of them stayed with local African American families. They were joined by clergy, attorneys, and medical and nursing professionals. Among other issues, the students were determined to help residents register to vote. It was a time of terrible tensions, where homes and churches were burned and people were hurt. Americans across the country were made aware of the events by the national news coverage. Tragically, three young civil rights workers lost their lives in the turmoil near Phila-delphia, Mississippi.

On July 7, 1964, President Lyndon B. Johnson signed into law the landmark Civil Rights Act of 1964. The act outlawed discrimination in public places and mandated integration of public schools. The legislation also banned dis-crimination in employment based on race, color, religion, sex, or national origin. A year later, on August 6, 1965, President Johnson signed the Voting Rights Act, which outlawed literacy tests. The efforts of those involved in Freedom Summer helped to enact this law. While the Twenty-fourth Amendment (rati-fied on January 23, 1964) abolished poll taxes in federal elec-tions, it took further action by the U.S. Supreme Court, which ruled on March 24, 1966, that poll taxes were unconstitu-tional for state and local elections. And while American males were guaranteed the right to vote by the Fifteenth Amendment (February 3, 1870), which stated that federal and state gov-ernments cannot deny American men the right to vote based on race, color, or being a former slave, this was not always enforced. Fifty years later, the Nineteenth Amendment that was ratified in 1920 gave all American women the right to vote, regardless of race. However, this amendment was not enforced either. It took nearly one hundred years, when the Voting Rights Act was signed, for all African Americans to be able to exercise their right to vote.

The year 1966 continued to bring struggles for Afri-can Americans in Canton. James Meredith, who success-fully integrated the University of Mississippi on October 1, 1962, under the protection of thousands of federal troops ordered by President Kennedy, desired to do more to com-bat racism, which was still very much a problem. On June 5, 1966, he decided to walk alone from Memphis to Jackson, the capital of Mississippi, making a journey of well over 200 miles to show support for voter registration. On the second day of his walk, he was shot and wounded by a white sniper from Memphis. In response, on June 23, 1966, thousands of marchers came to Canton to demonstrate solidarity with Meredith, in an event known as the March Against Fear. The city refused to allow the marchers to stay on public school property, so Father Mikschl offered the church property as a campsite. Over the course of three days, civil rights leaders, including Dr. Martin Luther King Jr., Stokely Carmichael, and Andrew Young, among others, spoke in the school gym. James Meredith's plan was realized when 15,000 thousand people assembled in Jackson and more than 2,500 African Americans were registered to vote during the march.

Besides church officials and those from outside of Mississippi, there were those in the community who discretely or otherwise worked for civil rights, knowing that they risked their own life and the lives of their family members. Their personal property was also at risk, as the burning or other destruction of homes and businesses occurred frequently. Mr. C. O. Chinn, Sr., a Canton resident and African American business owner, risked white ire by allowing civil rights workers to meet in his Community Pride grocery store and in his café. His actions jeopardized these and his other businesses. However, Mr. Chinn was not one to shy away from danger. Rather, he was known as a pistol-packing, self-proclaimed protector who stood up to the racial injustices of his time. He offered armed protection to workers from the Congress of Racial Equality (CORE) and others who were working to register voters. He and his wife were actively involved in the March Against Fear events. His bravery was not without struggle and sacrifice, though, as he ended up losing much of his property and served time in prison. Mr. Chinn is remembered as a leader in the civil rights movement in

Canton. His son and daughter-in-law and their family are longtime members of Holy Child Jesus Church.

While it is important to know and remember the injustices inflicted because of race, it is also important to be aware of and share stories of good people in the South who tried to do right things. Despite slavery, segregation, and the host of indignities inflicted on African Americans, there were occasionally small glimmers of hope. The "Salt Wagon Story" is an example where southerners overcame prejudices and mistrust, and eventually Sister Thea's family directly benefited.

In Kentucky, in the 1820s, a sixteen-year-old white youth named Samuel Meharry lost control of the salt wagon he was driving, and it went into a ditch. He was unhurt, but he had no way of getting help as it was soon to be dark. He observed a cabin and decided to walk over to it. Not knowing what he wanted or whether his intentions were honorable, the recently freed African American family who lived there offered him food and a place to spend the night. They had to be especially careful as bounty hunters were often looking for freed slaves. In the morning daylight, they helped young Samuel right his wagon, and the youth went on his way. He promised one day to repay the family's kindness and hospitality. Years later, Samuel and his four brothers kept that promise when they donated $30,000 and property to fund what would eventually become Meharry Medical College in Nashville, Dr. Bowman's alma mater. Today, Meharry medical students remember the altruistic actions in this story by operating the Salt Wagon Clinic. The student-run clinic provides free medical and dental care for Nashville residents in need, under the supervision of physicians and dentists. Dr. Bowman would undoubtedly be pleased.

Chapter 5

A WIDER WORLD

Leaving Wisconsin for graduate school in Washington, D.C., opened the doors for many new experiences for Sister Thea. In June 1966, when she enrolled at The Catholic University of America, she met students from across the country, and from many different countries. These students brought their diverse backgrounds to the university.

Washington, D.C., attracts people from all over the world. Prior to her move, Sister Thea had lived in the segregated South and in the insular city of La Crosse. Now, as a graduate student, she was exposed to many cultures. The presence of embassies and international organizations added to the diversity. There are also multiple universities, including Howard University, one of the historically black colleges and universities (HBCUs). In 1968, Sister Thea would be invited to speak at Howard. The universities offered classes, lectures, exchange programs, and cultural events. The presence of multiple museums with their exhibits and programs also added to the city's cultural vitality.

Sister Thea met and interacted for the first time with African American professionals, who worked in the public and private sectors. Through her interactions, she saw the opportunities that were available to educated African Americans that she had not previously experienced. Nevertheless, discrimination existed even in the nation's capital.

During the time that Sister Thea was in Washington, D.C., changes were occurring in the Church as a result of the Second Vatican Council (1962–65). The Council, convened by Pope John XXIII, called for a general reform of the liturgy, and was continued by Pope Paul VI. Incidentally, both conveners were eventually declared to be saints, or canonized. Some of the changes that resulted from the Council included that the priest would face the people, rather than east with his back to the assembly, and the laity were permitted a more participatory role. The language of the Mass could also now be in the local language of the people, rather than in Latin, which is still the official language of the Church. Over the years, the number of languages that Masses are celebrated in has increased greatly. In the Archdiocese of Washington, for example, Masses are celebrated in more than twenty languages, and in the Archdiocese of Los Angeles, they are celebrated in more than forty languages.

Another change as a result of the Council was the introduction in some parishes of cultural elements in their liturgies. Those parishes with mostly African American parishioners began to embrace a more Afrocentric form of worship. The timing of these changes also corresponded with many events and actions of the civil rights movement, as well as the rising black consciousness among African Americans.

The African influence in liturgy was experienced in the presence of West African drums, and in liturgical dance and movement. That more participatory and expressive form of worship attracted Sister Thea and other worshippers. Many of these churches also embraced African influences in art, statues, and decor. The vestments (garments worn by the clergy) were made from Kente prints and other African designs. Sister Thea experienced new ways of worshipping that she had not previously known. The churches she attended in Mississippi and in Wisconsin embraced a more Eurocentric liturgy, with European influences in art, music, and vestments.

Also, following the Second Vatican Council, some religious orders began to consider changes in the garments that they wore. After consideration, the FSPA adopted a modified street-length habit and veil in the late 1960s. Sister Thea embraced the new habit. In the 1970s, the FSPA order, among others, determined that they would wear secular clothing rather than the modified habit. Instead of separating themselves in appearance, they chose to dress more like the people they serve. The FSPA members continued to wear their congregational rings, and they wore their medals either on a chain or as a pin with their secular clothes.

In 1968, as Sister Thea began full-time graduate studies, she moved from the convent, where she had been living, to a graduate school hall on campus. She had a strong interest in Sir (St.) Thomas More (1478–1535), an accomplished English lawyer, writer, scholar, member of Parliament, and the Lord High Chancellor. He wrote the book *Utopia* in 1516, about an ideal society without greed, corruption, or power struggles. Sister Thea chose an early work of More's, his 1503 poem "A Rueful Lamentation on the Death of Queen Elizabeth," as the subject of her master's thesis, which was very well-received. She earned a master of arts degree in English from the Graduate School of Arts and Sciences at CUA in 1969.

During her time at CUA, Sister Thea was invited to speak at nearby Howard University. During her presentation, she spoke of the history of African Americans and education, and the need for new leadership among young, educated African Americans, particularly after the death of Dr. Martin Luther King Jr. The need for African Americans to pursue education was something that Sister Thea felt very passionately about and that would be a recurring theme for her. She knew that education was the key to a successful future and that civic engagement and social change depended not just on passionate leaders but also on articulate and persuasive leaders, who could engage in civil discourse.

A new opportunity arose for Sister Thea in 1970, when a member of the Sisters of Mercy community in Pittsburgh invited women's religious orders to send African American sisters to a gathering hosted by the Mercy community. Sister Thea attended and became one of the founding members of what became the National Black Sisters' Conference. The initial invitation brought together 150 black sisters from 76 religious orders. These sisters would now be part of a wider, national community of African American women religious that could offer friendship and support to each other. Over time, they and other African American Catholic groups, such as seminarians and clergy, worked together to better advocate for their needs and for those of African Americans in the Church. In the 1970s and 1980s, many dioceses opened ministry offices to better serve the needs of African American Catholics.

Sister Thea continued her studies at CUA from 1969 to 1972 as she pursued a doctoral degree so that she could teach at the college or university level. She taught a course on black literature for two semesters at CUA during the 1970–71 school year, which tied together her rising interest in cultural awareness and her love of literature. The course attracted both black and white students. Black studies classes began in the late 1960s and grew significantly in number. The first program in black studies began at San Francisco State University in 1968.

During the 1971–72 school year, Sister Thea returned to La Crosse, where she taught at her alma mater, Viterbo College, while she continued to work on her dissertation. During her time at Viterbo, she formed a diverse musical group of students, including those she brought from Canton, who were studying at the college. Known as the Hallelujah Singers, they sang spirituals and gospel songs at educational, religious, and community venues.

Sister Thea's continued interest in Sir Thomas More led her to select one of his later works, *A Dialogue of Comfort against Tribulation*, as the subject of her dissertation for her doctoral degree. It was written during More's fifteen-month imprisonment in the Tower of London. As a fierce defender of Catholic orthodoxy, he could not abide by King Henry VIII's divorce from Catherine of Aragon and was imprisoned. Sister Thea was particularly attracted to More's use of rhetoric to explain his beliefs and actions. She would adopt some of his techniques in her own speeches and writings in the years to come.

In 1972, Sister Thea was awarded a PhD in English Language, Literature, and Linguistics. She was pleased with the education she received at CUA and with the support from faculty members during her years of study.

Following the award of her degree, Sister Thea's parents acknowledged her significant accomplishment by presenting her with a trip abroad. On June 20, 1972, Sister Thea joined other FSPA sisters who were scheduled to travel overseas. They spent about three weeks visiting several European countries, including Germany, Austria, Italy, Greece, and France. In Italy, she had the opportunity to visit many sites that were meaningful to her, including the Vatican, Viterbo (the Italian town and namesake of Viterbo College and the St. Rose of Viterbo Convent), and Assisi, the birthplace of St. Francis of Assisi.

Sister Thea completed her trip with her highly anticipated enrollment in a three-week seminar at the University of Oxford in England. Before returning home, she spent two days in London, where she visited some of the famous landmarks related to Sir Thomas More, including the Tower of London.

The graduation trip enabled Sister Thea to experience firsthand European and English culture and life. She found it to be an invaluable experience to personally see many of the places she had studied that had played an important role in the English literature she favored. Sister Thea, with her engaging personality and presence, met many people and thoroughly enjoyed her time. She was particularly happy at Oxford, where she interacted with the international student body. Grateful to her parents, she kept them informed of her journey through regular post cards, which chronicled her adventures. Her parents corresponded with her as well.

Upon Sister Thea's return to the United States, she began teaching at Viterbo College as an English professor. She taught English Language and Literature. She subsequently became chair of the English Department. Sister Thea taught at Viterbo College until 1978. She reached out to students from the Wisconsin Winnebago Tribe (now Ho-Chunk Nation of Wisconsin) and to international students. She taught a range of courses, such as Composition and Literature, Shakespeare for Theatregoers, and Black American Literature.

In 1975, Sister Thea offered a course on Native American literature, a subject which was also of increasing interest. She brought in a Native American couple from the

Wisconsin Winnebago Tribe to help teach the class and to ensure that the subject was taught with accuracy and sensitivity. The course work included topics such as Winnebago writings, poetry, and history. There were also field trips to select Wisconsin sites. With the help of grant funding, the wider college community was invited to experience some of the cultural traditions through an evening of song, traditional dances, and readings. Tribal members performed the Snake, Hoop, Swan, and Peace Pipe dances.

All her efforts in the classroom made Sister Thea a popular teacher who continued to embrace many of the same ideals she had held and practices she had used in her early teaching days. She engaged her students through interactive and participatory endeavors. She took students who were studying William Faulkner and Eudora Welty to southern sites, including Oxford and Jackson, in Mississippi, to learn more about these writers in the places that influenced their works. Those studying William Shakespeare had the opportunity to see Shakespearean performances in various U.S. cities, as well as in Stratford, Ontario, and Stratford-upon-Avon, in England. Sister Thea included trips to her hometown of Canton, where many students experienced for the first time the realities of life in the Deep South. They were introduced to African American culture by staying with African American host families. Sister Thea's emphasis on experiential learning gave her students new perspectives. Because of her teaching methods, she was a successful and sought-after teacher. To her students, she was a caring, devoted, and supportive teacher, who brought enormous vitality to the classroom.

Sister Thea embraced life to the fullest. Her keen intellect, unbridled energy and enthusiasm, and desire to expose her students to so many aspects of life kept her constantly challenged and engaged. She wanted her students to broaden their horizons and experience all that life has to offer, just as she had. She was also a demanding teacher as she sought to draw out the best in each of her students.

As more and more people were exposed to Sister Thea, she was invited to speak and lecture in many places. Her interest in cultural awareness was often the subject of her presentations. She enjoyed the opportunities that these invitations provided her, particularly in being able to share the important message that she sought to convey about the need for the awareness and acceptance of other cultures.

During her career in education, Sister Thea had the unique opportunity to teach at various grade levels. She relished each of her experiences and gained as much from the students in her classes as they did from her. In an FSPA interview in May 1988, she said, "The experience of teaching has impacted the most on my life. Teaching in grade school, high school, college, and university, I realize, as I have grown older, how many of my own personal and emotional needs have been met in the classroom and how much I've learned from my students."

In 1978, after completing the summer session, Sister Thea left La Crosse to return to Canton. Her aging parents needed support and, as an only child, Sister Thea, with per-mission of her order, desired to return to her hometown to help care for them. She looked forward to returning to the South, to the place of her birth, and to the community she knew so well.

Chapter 6

RETURNING HOME

When Sister Thea returned to Canton, she was offered a position by Bishop Joseph B. Brunini, who had succeeded Bishop Gerow. Bishop Brunini, the first native-born bishop in Mississippi, was installed in January 1968. Bishops customarily have a coat of arms with a motto of their choice. Bishop Brunini selected "God and Neighbor," from the Great Commandment (Matt 22:36–40) as his episcopal motto.

In the Parable of the Good Samaritan (Luke 10:25–37), Jesus responds to the lawyer's question, "Who is my neighbor?" by telling the story of a Samaritan, who showed love, kindness, and mercy to a person in need, irrespective of nationality, religion, or personal or financial cost. Bishop Brunini's choice for his motto was reflective of him and his beliefs, as he was known for his kindness and compassion, and his commitment to civil rights.

In 1970, Bishop Brunini played an important role in the formation of the interfaith Mississippi Religious Leadership Conference and served as the first chair. He demonstrated his commitment to African Americans through his support of St. Augustine Seminary in Bay St. Louis. He not only supported the ordinations of African Americans but had an African American auxiliary bishop, Joseph Lawson Howze, who would later become the first bishop of the new Diocese of Biloxi. In 1977, the Diocese of Natchez-Jackson was divided into two dioceses: the Diocese of Jackson, led by Bishop Brunini, and the Diocese of Biloxi, led by Bishop Howze.

Bishop Brunini had a strong commitment to the Mississippi Band of Choctaw Indians, who are native to the state. They reside on 35,000 acres in ten counties. Since 1944, the Missionary Servants of the Most Holy Trinity, the same religious order that started Holy Child Jesus Mission in Canton, have staffed Holy Rosary Indian Mission in the Tucker community of the Choctaw reservation (near Philadelphia, Mississippi), and its two mission churches in Choctaw and Conehatta. These are places where they serve Choctaw Native Americans in Mississippi. (The order was originally invited to serve at the request of Bishop Gerow.) Bishop Brunini was also instrumental in the establishment of a mission in the city of Saltillo, in northern Mexico, which serves impoverished, mountainous villages.

As Bishop Brunini offered a position to Sister Thea in 1978, he was aware of the risks he was taking by hiring an African American woman in the culture in which they lived. However, he was also cognizant of the many benefits that her employment could bring to the diocese. He envisioned her as a valuable resource in diocesan efforts to promote intercultural awareness. She was not only a native of the state, but was an excellent and well-respected scholar and teacher, who for many years was teaching and speaking on the topic of cultural awareness. She also had her own personal experiences in this area, particularly while in La Crosse at St. Rose Convent and at Blessed Sacrament School. Sister

Thea's title was Diocesan Consultant (later Director) for Intercultural Awareness for the Diocese of Jackson. The position was supported by an annual Catholic Extension grant that funds mission dioceses.

In her position, Sister Thea designed a variety of programs for diverse audiences, including children, teens, and adults, to break down the existing barriers between cultures. She wanted participants to realize that, regardless of one's race or ethnicity, everyone is "God's child." She believed that "all God's children have something to give to each other."

Sister Thea surmised that if people were provided with opportunities to know each other as individuals, they would recognize their shared humanity and feel less threatened by their differences. As part of her outreach, she initiated efforts not only with black and white communities, but with Hispanic, Native American, and Asian communities as well.

As someone who loved children and enjoyed interacting with them, Sister Thea was truly in her element using her gifts when she was involved with children. She took her one-woman show to multiple places, and before audiences of children, she told stories and sang songs, and had the children join her, and she recited poetry and performed dramatic presentations. Sister Thea wanted children to know the stories from the scriptures and, in her presentations, drew her young audiences into the stories by her realistic portrayals. By engaging children in interactive performances, she fulfilled one of her own beliefs: "You can get a child to remember anything if you make the learning fun." She may have recalled how she and the other students at Holy Child Jesus School were captivated by the religion lessons taught by the parish priests so many years ago.

As the tall, willowy sister stood before her young audiences, her teaching brought to life Moses, Joshua, and

Daniel, and other biblical figures. On the one hand, she enthralled white students who may not have encountered an African American sister before or one who engaged the children as she did. Her presentations also provided these children with the opportunity to see an African American sister as a representative of the Church. She said, "What the students see speaks more powerfully than what they hear or read." For African American children, on the other hand, Sister Thea was someone who could model the Church for them. They could aspire to be someone like her. She showed them that they could be both black and Catholic, and that there are many places at God's table. Furthermore, in the African American tradition, she taught them the stories from the scriptures that some of their ancestors had learned from oral tradition. She taught all the children the meaning of the songs, just as Mother Ricker had taught her. She believed the children sang better when they understood what they were singing. Sister Thea knew how important it was that the children know "who you are and whose you are."

The dramatic and musical presentations accomplished another goal as well. They reached a variety of learners, since they involved so many of the senses. Sister Thea reached the visual learner because of the imagery she presented. She reached the auditory learner not only through the stories she told and how she expressed them, but also through the songs the children sang with her. She also reached the kinesthetic learner through her hands-on experiential learning and movement. No one was left unmoved or untouched after one of Sister Thea's performances.

According to Sister Thea, everyone, including children, had a "responsibility to the Church." As she said of children, "By your baptism, you are called to preach and to teach. You're called by your baptism to worship and praise.

You're called by your baptism to serve, to help somebody, to feed somebody, to love somebody. You're never too young." Sister Thea truly felt that if parents and teachers could instill in children these beliefs, there would be profound changes in the Church and in society. As a child, she learned that helping others brought joy and peace.

Sister Thea organized a children's choir that performed at schools, churches, and community events. Once again, she saw that those children who had difficulty learning in school benefited from music. As she explained, "We try to use the music as a tool to teach subject matter, to teach poise and confidence, and to teach expression." She knew that music was an important tool to engage children and youth, to build self-esteem, and to enable them to embrace the gifts that God had given them.

In addition to programs for children, there were also programs for teenagers, teachers, and parents. She believed that "if our children are to be adequately prepared for life in a pluralistic, multiethnic, multicultural world, they must learn to understand and appreciate the basic religious traditions of the persons with whom they live and work." She offered an assembly program for elementary and high school students, and for parent and teacher groups, "Getting to Know You," where participants learned about their own culture and that of others through art and sharing stories. Through a communications workshop for junior and senior high school families and for parent and teacher groups, she strove to enhance communication among parents, teachers, and teens. As a former high school teacher, who "found high school teaching most taxing," she knew the importance of continually improving communication.

Sister Thea also led retreats, revivals, days of recollection, workshops, and programs for the liturgical seasons.

In a multicultural awareness day, "That All May Be One," which took place in December 1978, the year she began her position, the agenda included presentations by her and a professor from Tougaloo College, multiracial and multicultural panels, and a multicultural liturgy. Ethnic foods, an ethnic arts and crafts exhibit, Irish storytelling, and Filipino and Choctaw dances were also part of the program. Music was provided by the Choctaw Central Indian Music Chorus and by the Holy Child Jesus Gospel Choir. A type of singing common to Gaelic speaking areas of Ireland, Irish Lilt, was included as well.

To expand her outreach, Sister Thea offered programs for community events and other faith traditions. During one memorable presentation at a Presbyterian church in north Jackson, she concluded the one-hour program by having those in attendance stand, hold hands, and sing, "We Shall Overcome." This ending would come to be representative of her. The pastor recognized his congregation would long remember this evening.

In addition to presenting programs, Sister Thea was able to continue in academia by her involvement with the Institute of Black Catholic Studies at Xavier University of Louisiana in New Orleans, that began in the summer of 1980. The university was originally founded in 1915 by St. Katherine Drexel and the Sisters of the Blessed Sacrament as a secondary school. Xavier University is the only historically black, Catholic university in the United States. The Institute offers degrees and summer formation programs in fields to prepare clergy, religious, and laypeople to minister in the African American community. Sister Thea was a popular and dynamic instructor at the Institute from its beginning until 1988.

Prayer was a very important part of Sister Thea's life. Whether it included words, spirituals, or movement, it energized and brought comfort to her. She also embraced contemplative prayer, where one focuses on a word or phrase, or places oneself in a story or scene, such as from one of the four gospels. What was it like to be a part of the story or to be with Jesus at the cross? In a Lenten reflection for the Jackson diocesan newspaper that she dictated a few weeks before her death, she spoke of being at the cross with Jesus: "Watch as Jesus is sentenced by Pilate to Calvary, to see him rejected, mocked, spat upon, beaten, and forced to carry a heavy cross...to know Mary's anguish." She wanted people to be there with Jesus, to share the burden with him.

For Sister Thea, prayer needed to encompass gratitude. She believed that it is necessary to express gratitude to God for the blessings that we have received. Sister Thea also advocated that a way to increase intercultural awareness was to embrace different prayer forms, such as a Native American harvest prayer or an Asian body prayer.

Sister Thea embodied Franciscan spirituality. Like Bishop Brunini, she felt that it was important to follow the Great Commandment in her life and ministry. Sister Thea loved God and God's people. She particularly desired to help those in need. She never forgot where she came from or the people in her community. She saw the devastation that segregation brought to African Americans and knew the importance of treating everyone with compassion, respect, and equality, and of offering to "help a brother, sister, or stranger." The scriptures were important to Sister Thea, and she tried to live her life in accordance with them. She radiated a joy of life that was contagious to those around her. She loved all of God's creation and, like St. Francis, particularly enjoyed birds. Perhaps their songs resonated with her.

Music plays a unique role in African American life, and, as Sister Thea said, "Music is life for the black community."

It is a felt experience, which speaks to the soul. She also believed that "singing is a legitimate way to get in touch with God and my neighbor." Sister Thea was raised by a mother who relished music and her childhood home was always "full of song." She particularly embraced the spirituals, which she learned as a child. The elders in Canton taught them to the children as a means of teaching "scripture and faith, and values and love, and dedication." They were continuing a long tradition.

Sister Thea recognized the importance of the spirituals and endeavored to keep the stories of the past alive. She included them in her performances and programs, as they tell the story of the African American experience, including the history and culture. For her and others, the spirituals offered "hope and consolation and joy." As she explained, "The songs of our people are the key to understanding our faith." No matter how difficult the trials and tribulations were for African Americans, their belief in God remained steadfast. They knew that God was not the source of the pain and suffering they experienced. In the fields, under a tree, or in attempting to escape to freedom, African Americans sang or carried a song in their hearts.

As the diocesan leadership changed, Sister Thea continued her intercultural efforts with Bishop William R. Houck, who succeeded Bishop Brunini as bishop of the Diocese of Jackson in April 1984. She had already worked with him because he had been appointed auxiliary bishop in March 1979.

As Sister Thea worked to develop awareness among people, she not unexpectedly experienced some resistance. Not everyone appreciated the changes that she proposed. She had to confront issues among both white and black Catholics in the diocese. Rather than actual resistance, some of the white Catholics were apathetic to her and her programs. As Bishop Houck said of the lack of interest among the white Catholics, "It was a challenge to see all people, especially whites, recognize the dignity of all people, especially in a culture where they thought they were superior." Bishop Houck knew that work needed to continue to ensure lasting change. As he observed, "We've changed laws. We still need to change hearts." As even Jesus experienced, that is much harder to do.

Some African American Catholics, including those who converted to Catholicism from other faith traditions, and those who had no previous religious affiliation, were content with their parishes and liturgies. They saw neither the need to increase their own awareness, nor the need to make changes in their parishes. They objected to some of the liturgical changes that Sister Thea proposed. Many were not familiar with Afrocentric influences and were concerned that she was leading them back to more Protestant traditions, particularly Baptist. Through the Church, they had learned that "the European way was better." Sister Thea believed some artwork found in Catholic churches, such as the Stations of the Cross or statues, might be appropriate in some Eurocentric churches but not in an African American church, since it did not reflect the culture. As a teacher, she knew that education and more preparation was needed before some changes would be accepted.

Chapter 7

A DIFFICULT YEAR

In March 1984, Sister Thea faced a new challenge when she was diagnosed with breast cancer. The year was a particularly difficult one for her as she underwent treatment and tried to care for her parents, who were both ill. They would die within a short period of time of each other by the end of the year. Despite aggressive treatment for her cancer, Sister Thea continued her work. Rather than worrying about her prognosis, she decided, "What matters is how I love, how I laugh and listen, and how I communicate the Good News."

The following year, in August 1985—and thanks to the generosity of many people who cared about her—Sister Thea was able to travel to Africa for the forty-third International Eucharistic Congress in Nairobi, Kenya. She joined Pope St. John Paul II and thousands of participants, who came from forty-three countries for the first Eucharistic Congress held in Africa. In addition to visiting Kenya in East Africa, she also traveled to Zimbabwe in the South, and Nigeria in West Africa to visit friends. Her trip provided her with a greater understanding of the devotion and worship of African Catholics, and how they contribute to the universal

Church. Sister Thea was thrilled to be welcomed by so many people who were eager to share African culture with her as she explored her own "roots."

On May 3, 1987, she appeared on the CBS news program *60 Minutes* with journalist Mike Wallace. Her segment was filmed over a two-year period at various places that held significance for her, including Canton, Jackson, New Orleans, and Washington, D.C. Mr. Wallace was deeply touched by the time he spent with Sister Thea. The program, which was aired three times, and once more after her death, increased Sister Thea's visibility and helped make her known across the country.

Her increasing stature brought Sister Thea many invitations to speak and work with other dioceses and groups around the country. She accepted engagements to multiple events from coast-to-coast. As was her custom, Sister Thea dressed in African attire for her presentations. She felt most comfortable wearing garments that reflected her ancestry. The bright and eye-catching fabrics reflected her joyfulness.

Sister Thea was also an organizer of the sixth Black Catholic Congress, which was held May 21–24, 1987, at The Catholic University of America. The first Black Catholic Congress, founded by Daniel Rudd, was held in January 1889 at St. Augustine's Church in Washington, D.C. The 1987 Congress was the first one held since 1894. At this congress, the *Pastoral Plan of Action* for the African American community was developed. Participants agreed that in the future they would meet every five years.

In the fall of 1987, Sister Thea served as a contributor and editor for GIA Publications for *Lead Me, Guide Me: The African American Catholic Hymnal*, which contains songs and psalms for liturgical use. Her close friend Bishop James P. Lyke, OFM, auxiliary bishop of Cleveland (later archbishop of Atlanta), oversaw the compilation of this hymnal. The hymnal was dedicated to Father Clarence R. Rivers of the Archdiocese of Cincinnati, for his enormous efforts in liturgical renewal, particularly in the black Catholic liturgical movement.

In January 1988, after being in remission from her cancer for four years, Sister Thea learned that her cancer had returned and spread to other parts of her body. As it became increasingly difficult for her to walk, she was given a wheelchair by her friend Dan Rooney, owner of the Pittsburgh Steelers. Mr. Rooney is credited with playing a major role in establishing the rule that NFL teams must interview at least one minority candidate to fill vacancies for manager or head coach—the "Rooney Rule." He met Sister Thea in La Crosse in 1985.

Wishing to be active, despite needing a wheelchair, she remarked, "I intend to live until I die." And she did, especially continuing to sing until she no longer could. Singing was a balm to ease her pain. There was not much that could keep Sister Thea from breaking out in song. She sang when she was happy, when she wanted to teach a lesson or to convey a message, or when in distress, particularly during a difficult medical procedure. Singing was her lifeblood and it conveyed all her emotions.

In September 1988, Sister Thea fulfilled her desire to return to the African continent when she traveled to Tanzania in East Africa to conduct workshops for Maryknoll sisters on the topic "Racism in Ministry." Because she was too weak to travel alone, she was accompanied by a small entourage, including her good friend and companion, who had also taught at Holy Child Jesus School, Sister Dorothy Ann Kundinger, FSPA. Sister Thea was never one to surrender and knew that much work remained to be accomplished.

In 1988, she recorded an audiocassette of fifteen spirituals, *Sister Thea: Songs of My People*, in Boston with Krystal Records of the Daughters of St. Paul. She was ill and physically struggled to complete the project. The following year, she produced an audiocassette of Christmas spirituals, *Sister Thea: Round the Glory Manger*, also by Krystal Records.

On June 17, 1989, Sister Thea was invited to address the U.S. bishops at their spring general assembly at Seton Hall University in South Orange, New Jersey. She was there as a member of the Committee on Black Catholics to urge the bishops to support the *Pastoral Plan of Action*. Facing the bishops in her wheelchair, Sister Thea began her presentation by asking, "What does it mean to be black in the church and society?" She immediately answered her own question by singing the spiritual "Sometimes I Feel Like a Motherless Child," which describes the powerlessness and trials of the slaves. It was important to her that the bishops be cognizant of the needs in African American communities, and the song reinforced her message. Because she saw song as a form of prayer, she wanted the bishops to understand what was in her heart. She believed that African American Catholics needed to feel that they belonged to the Church and that their culture was welcomed and appreciated. Challenging the bishops to recognize and accept the contributions and spirituality of black Catholics, she told them, "We are called to walk together in new ways," as they listened intently to her. At the end of her presentation, she invited them to stand, lock their arms, and join her in singing, "We Shall Overcome." The *Pastoral Plan of Action* was unanimously approved at the bishop's fall general assembly in November 1989.

As Sister Thea knew, people of faith come from many different traditions, cultures, and backgrounds. She told the bishops, "I bring my whole history, my traditions, my experience, my culture, my African American song and dance, and gesture and movement, and teaching and preaching, and healing and responsibility as gift to the Church." African American worship is holistic and may include vocal expressions and affirmations, such as "Amen," "Hallelujah," or "Thank you, Jesus" that are not commonly found in a Eurocentric Mass. It was important to Sister Thea that people understand that there is room in the Church for everyone.

As many people learned, it was as futile to try to subdue the exuberant Sister Thea as it was to keep a bird from singing. Her friend and classmate Sister Charlene Smith, FSPA, experienced that as she valiantly tried to stop her from verbally expressing herself during the homily at Mass at St. Matthew's Cathedral in Washington, D.C. Sister Thea quickly reminded her, "Stay open to the spirit."

Sister Thea knew that Jesus called all people to follow him: ordinary people from diverse walks of life, including those who fish or collect taxes, have visual impairments or disease, have persecuted him, or are women. He demonstrated through countless examples that all people are welcome in his kingdom, even modern-day disciples who verbally respond to the homily.

To Sister Thea's disappointment, she was unable to teach in the summer program in 1989 at the Institute for Black Catholic Studies at Xavier University due to her declining health. Her devoted students and members of the Institute community instead traveled by bus on July 4 to see her. They gathered at Holy Child Jesus Church and showered her with the love and friendship that she had given them.

Sister Thea sent form letters to friends and colleagues to keep them apprised of her condition, as well as of her work and travels. In her letters, she identified the places that she had visited since the previous letter. The number of places could easily make a well person weary, let alone someone who was quite ill. In the first five months of 1989, she traveled to twenty cities out of state and two in Mississippi. From June through November 1989, she visited fifteen places around the country, plus four more in Mississippi. Despite the obstacles she faced, she continued to keep up her frenetic pace. As Bishop Houck said, "She had a willingness to share herself with others." While work kept her occupied and contributing, prayer and the scriptures gave her peace. She remembered the importance of expressing gratitude in prayer. A simple prayer that she now embraced was "Thank you, Lord."

During her years in Mississippi, in addition to her work, travels, and teaching, Sister Thea continued to pursue her love of literature. She was an expert on William Shakespeare and William Faulkner. A Mississippi novelist and short story writer, Faulkner was the recipient of the 1949 Nobel Prize in Literature and the Pulitzer Prize in 1955 and, posthumously, in 1962. He was a prolific writer who authored nineteen novels.

Sister Thea was a longtime presenter at the annual Faulkner and Yoknapatawpha Conference, which drew an international audience. The conference was named after the writer's fictional Yoknapatawpha County in Oxford, Mississippi. The topic for the sixteenth conference, which was held July 30 to August 4, 1989, was "Faulkner and Religion." Sister Thea, accompanied by an eleven-member local choir, sang spirituals interspersed with readings for her presentation, "Faulkner and That Ole Time Religion." She believed that Faulkner not only understood but admired the "ole time religion" of African Americans. Her scholarly presentation led other contributors to reconsider their own views and well-planned presentations. Sister Thea was particularly drawn to Faulkner, as he expressed his beliefs on segregation and race-related topics in his home state, which led her to say, "Faulkner helped me to understand the southern mentality." In 1955, he denounced the murder of young Emmett Till, as well as the practice of segregation. He advocated "moderation and patience," however, and did not approve of the intrusion of the federal government, a sentiment that he shared with many other southerners.

Despite the pain and suffering that Sister Thea experienced, she was determined to proceed with her life. Work invigorated her, particularly when she was engaged with children. She fell back on the words and sayings that the elders had taught her and the spirituals that she had learned as a young child. She said, "If I can sing, I can cope."

Chapter 8

A LIFE WELL LIVED

Sister Thea died of metastatic breast cancer at her family home on March 30, 1990, six years after her initial diagnosis. She was in the company of her loyal friend and faithful companion, Sister Dorothy Ann, and some of her closest friends, who gathered to be near during her final days. Upon learning of her death, the bells at Viterbo College rang fifty-two times, one for each year of her life.

While not unexpected, Sister Thea's death brought enormous sorrow to many people in the United States and abroad who had come to know, love, and respect her for all that she did for the Church, for increasing cultural awareness, not just in Mississippi, but across the country, and for opening the eyes, ears, and hearts of the students she had taught. Just as she grew in awareness from her own life experiences, education, and travel, Sister Thea sought to bring the wider world to others. She knew that the Church was large enough to encompass the cultural traditions of all its members, including African American Catholics.

Upon learning of Sister Thea's death, Governor Ray Mabus of Mississippi sent a letter dated April 2, 1990, to the pastor of Holy Child Jesus Church expressing his condolences. Governor Mabus recognized the many years that Sister Thea had served the Church and the people of Mississippi, particularly the children.

A wake was held at Holy Child Jesus Church in Canton on April 2, where Sister Thea's beloved parish children's choir sang. The next day, a three-hour funeral Mass was celebrated at St. Mary's Church in west Jackson, the largest Catholic church that could hold the fifteen hundred people who had come from across the country. Regardless of their background, they came to remember, honor, and celebrate Sister Thea's life. The Mass was celebrated by Father Bede Abram, OFM, a friend and co-instructor at the Institute for Black Catholic Studies. The homilist was Father John E. Ford, ST, a close friend and a member of the order that started the Holy Child Jesus Mission. Similar to when Sister Thea told the students at Howard University in 1968 that new leadership was needed, particularly after the death of Dr. King, Father Ford told those gathered, "We must also find ways to imitate this irreplaceable woman." While neither Sister Thea nor Dr. King can truly be replaced, leaders are needed to continue their efforts.

Among the songs that Sister Thea chose for her funeral Mass, she selected one that she sang at her parents' funerals: "I've Done My Work." Other songs she chose included a favorite, "This Little Light of Mine," and "I'll Be Singing Up There." Local parishes contributed money and cakes to feed the hundreds of people who attended the repast following the funeral Mass.

Sister Thea was buried on April 4, 1990, at the historic Elmwood Cemetery in Memphis, which was established in 1852. It is a beautiful and expansive eighty-acre resting place, replete with sculptures, angels, trees, and gardens.

Sister Thea was buried next to her father's brother, Jamison, and her parents. Her friend, Bishop Lyke, led her committal service. Her gravestone was inscribed "Sr. Thea, 1937–1990" and the words she chose: "She tried." Before her death, she expressed the hope that on the day of judgment, she could say, "I have really tried; I have done my best."

Near Sister Thea's grave are the unmarked graves of more than three hundred unidentified slaves who were buried between 1852 and 1865. The monument to them is engraved with words from the spiritual "Oh Freedom," expressing the desire to die and be free—home with the Lord—rather than ever to be a slave.

Sister Thea led a full and remarkable life in her fifty-two years. During her life and posthumously, she was honored and recognized for the enormous contributions she made in so many areas, including the Church, education, and social justice.

In 1983, Sister Thea was the first person to receive the Diocese of La Crosse Justice and Peace award. In 1985, Viterbo College presented the Pope John XXIII Award for Distinguished Service to her and to Dan Rooney of the Pittsburgh Steelers, along with two others. In 1986, the National Black Sisters' Conference honored Sister Thea with the Harriet Tubman Award for Leadership with Black Catholics.

In 1988, Sister Thea was one of the fifty state recipients of the Courage Award given by the American Cancer Society. She traveled to Washington, D.C., to receive the award in a ceremony held in the Rose Garden of the White House.

On January 16, 1989, Sister Thea became the first recipient of the Sister Thea Bowman Justice Award from Bishop Topal Ministries in Spokane, Washington, for her work on justice in the United States. On March 26, 1989, she was presented with four awards. She received awards from President Ronald Reagan, Secretary of Education William Bennett, Wisconsin Congressman Steve Gunderson, and Wisconsin Governor Tommy G. Thompson. That same year, Sister Thea was recognized by the publication *U.S. Catholic* for her efforts on behalf of women in the Church.

In the summer of 1989, noted Mississippi artist, Marshall Bouldin, was commissioned by two anonymous donors to paint a formal portrait of Sister Thea. The beautiful painting, which exhibits so much of her radiance even while sick, hangs in the offices of the Diocese of Jackson.

In 1989, the Sister Thea Bowman Black Catholic Educational Foundation (now Sister Thea Bowman Foundation) was established by Dr. Leonard and Mary Lou Jennings with consultation by Sister Thea. The foundation raises money to enable African American students to attend Catholic universities. Sister Thea knew from her own experience and as a teacher how important education was and what it could offer to young people.

On February 12, 1990, Sister Thea was one of five honorees of the University of Mississippi's fourth annual Awards of Distinction of 1990. She was awarded the 1990 University of Notre Dame Laetare Award shortly before her death. The award was established in 1883 and is the highest honor given to an American Catholic. It was presented posthumously at commencement on May 20, 1990. She joined past notable recipients, including President John F. Kennedy (1961) and Dorothy Day (1972), a social activist, Catholic convert, and cofounder of the Catholic Worker Movement. Also in 1990, Sister Thea received the Bishop Carroll T. Dozier Award for Peace and Justice. Bishop Dozier, founder of Pax Christi, was the first bishop of Memphis.

Sister Thea was also recognized by several educational institutions, which awarded her honorary degrees.

She was awarded her first honorary doctorate from Regis College in Weston, Massachusetts, on May 21, 1988. Other institutions that honored her include Boston College in Chestnut Hill, Massachusetts; Clarke College in Dubuque, Iowa; Xavier University of Louisiana in New Orleans; Sacred Heart University in Fairfield, Connecticut; Viterbo College in La Crosse, Wisconsin; Georgetown University in Washington, D.C.; and Spring Hill College in Mobile, Alabama.

Art is another way that Sister Thea has been commemorated. St. Benedict the African Church in Chicago, with its renowned architecture and art, has beautiful stained glass windows created by local artist David Lee Csicsko, including the "Four Strong Black Women." The women paired together, are Harriet Tubman and Sojourner Truth, and Sister Thea and Rosa Parks. The selection of Sister Thea with the other three women, who have such historical significance, demonstrates her great importance and contributions, particularly among African Americans. She would be most pleased that this church was designed to reflect the history and culture of its parishioners, including the building, which is in the shape of an African hut. The first Mass at the church was celebrated on Mother's Day in 1990. The stained glass windows of the women were dedicated in October 2002. St. Benedict Moor, the son of African slaves, was a Franciscan friar (lay brother) and is the patron saint of African Americans.

Another very special honor was bestowed on Sister Thea when she was chosen as one of four diverse "artists of faith" memorialized in hand-carved German statues gracing Dudley Birder Hall at St. Norbert College, De Pere, Wisconsin. Birder Hall, formerly St. Boniface Church, was renovated to be used primarily for musical performances, and was dedicated on February 14, 2013. The statues were commissioned and installed in January 2015. Sister Thea is depicted in African clothing holding a copy of *Lead Me, Guide Me: The African American Catholic Hymnal*. A nearby quote of Sister Thea's says, "If each one of us would light the candle, we've got a tremendous light." She recognized the impact that each person could make. Each of the honorees was elected to represent a different artistic form. Sister Thea was selected for liturgical dance, King David for music, St. Hildegard of Bingen for visual arts, and C. S. Lewis for literature.

Several institutions and organizations honor Sister Thea with awards in her name. Providence College in Rhode Island recognizes a graduating senior who most embodies the life and work of Sister Thea and has worked for inclusivity on campus. Catholic Charities of the Diocese of Cleveland honors African American women in recognition of their leadership and service.

In 2014, St. Joseph's University, a Jesuit university in Philadelphia, initiated The Sister Thea Bowman, FSPA, Distinguished Lecture Series. The annual lecture highlights research efforts of an African American woman.

The mayor of La Crosse declared March 30, 2015, "Sister Thea Bowman Day." She was recognized for her contributions to the La Crosse community on the twenty-fifth anniversary of her death.

On March 24, 2018, Sister Thea was honored as one of five "women of courage" by Connecting the Dots Foundation, a Jackson foundation that supports organizations in many ways, including raising money for scholarships. Sister Thea was selected for fostering "diversity in the faith community."

There are numerous entities that bear the name of Sister Thea. Some of these include day care centers, schools, medical facilities, and senior housing. Her name is also attached to gospel choirs, dance teams, and sports teams.

At Sister Thea Bowman Catholic School in Jackson, students are taught some of the same lessons that Sister Thea learned as a child. As one young student recalled, "She taught me to have perseverance, and that I should never give up—even if I am close to death, I should keep on pushing myself to try." Perseverance was one of the character traits taught by the elders in Canton, Mississippi.

Numerous individuals have devised their own ways to acknowledge Sister Thea. Brother Michael McGrath, OSF, has written a book and designed beautiful artwork depicting her, including a digital painting, "Brother Sun, Sister Thea," which portrays St. Francis of Assisi and Sister Thea. He also composed the presentation "This Little Light of Mine: An Art & Music Celebration of Sr. Thea Bowman." Mary Queen Donnelly, a Canton native, has written a play, "Thea's Turn." Several books have been written about Sister Thea. She is also remembered in her hometown at the Canton Multicultural Center and Museum, which has an exhibit on its native daughter.

While Sister Thea would be honored by all the awards and accolades given to her, she would be happiest to know that African American Catholics and other minorities and their cultures were welcomed in the Church. She would not want anyone to "feel like a motherless child."

Despite laws and increased cultural awareness, the United States is still plagued by racial conflict and insensitivity, which the U.S. bishops have sought to address. In 1979, the bishops issued "Brothers and Sisters to Us: U.S. Catholic Bishops Pastoral Letter on Racism," in which they identified racism as a sin and presented several recommendations, including the need for a conversion or a change of heart. In September 1984, the ten African American bishops released their own pastoral letter on evangelization: "What We have Seen and Heard." Sister Thea served as a consultant on this document. Sadly, the events in our country over the past several years have called for a renewed effort by the bishops to confront the insidious effects of racism on God's people. In November 2018, the U.S. bishops approved a new letter, "Open Wide Our Hearts: The Enduring Call to Love—A Pastoral Letter against Racism." In this new document, leaders of the Church address individual and institutional racism, including that which may be present in church communities and in society. They acknowledge that "Racism still profoundly affects our culture and has no place in our hearts." There is once again a call for a conversion to combat this lingering evil. The pastoral letter identifies three groups that are targeted, including Native Americans, African Americans, and Hispanics. The bishops recognized the contributions of Sister Thea and others who worked to bring the faith to African Americans.

The year 2018 proved to be an important one concerning another evil that is a tragic part of American history. The National Memorial for Peace and Justice, dedicated to the victims of lynching, opened on April 26, 2018, in Montgomery, Alabama. Through unique sculpture and jars of soil from lynching sites, the memorial seeks to not only remember those who have lost their lives, but to educate future generations on these unconscionable acts. As the year came to an end, the Justice for Victims of Lynching Act of 2018 was passed by the U.S. Senate on December 19, 2018. The legislation recognized the more than 4,700 recorded lynchings that occurred between 1882 and 1968, the majority of whom were African American. Historically, Mississippi had the highest rate of lynching, followed by Georgia and Texas.

For all its historical and racial issues and economic and educational deprivations, Mississippi is still recognized in many areas. The state has produced some of the country's finest writers, including William Faulkner, Eudora Welty, Walker Percy, and Shelby Foote. Thomas "Tennessee" Williams, Willie Morris, Richard Wright, Stark Young, and Margaret Walker Alexander are also from Mississippi. Besides writers, Mississippi has produced its own civil rights leaders and organizers, including Medgar Evers and Fannie Lou Hamer. A small, segregated city, beset by poverty and racial injustice, produced a young girl who would embrace the God of a minority church in Mississippi, and grow up dedicated in service to God and others, and make lasting contributions.

Chapter 9
THE LEGACY OF SISTER THEA BOWMAN

In modern-day life, we need prophets, people who can open our minds and our hearts to see that there are many ways to interpret the world around us. Prophets call people out and help them to understand God's message. Dr. Martin Luther King Jr. was one. Both brave and bold, he too challenged the conventional wisdom of his time. He believed that people of different cultures and creeds could coexist and together could make lasting change. Sister Thea believed that "we're all called."

Sister Thea possessed an intellect and a desire that would lead her and guide her in the service of others. Her dedication to her principles enabled her to achieve her goals of understanding and respect, and love for one another, that would characterize her life. As an only child, she was encouraged and indulged, but was also expected to succeed. She was not afraid of challenges. Her view of the Catholic Church initially came from a young child's perspective, from white sisters, brothers, and priests who ministered in the Deep South at a time of intense segregation. She saw these representatives of the Church stand up for the rights of African Americans to be educated, to worship freely, and to live in a just and equal society. She also saw them address the broad needs of her community. Her world and her views began to expand because of their behavior and desire for justice. Through observing the good works that they performed in her community, she became a member of the Church at the age of nine.

Sister Thea's interaction with many different people, her advanced education and exposure to great literature, and her travels had a profound effect on her. These experiences also broadened her horizons and showed her the significant ethnic diversity in the world. She saw that the world was bigger than herself and her community. All of us need dreams. Seeing and realizing that there is a world outside of our own communities enables us to see that our dreams can be realized. God continues to call women and men, young and old, to lead lives of holiness and service. We need people who can challenge us to see and think and do things in other ways. The sisters, brothers, and priests in Canton showed young Bertha and the others that life could be different than what they had experienced and witnessed. Even at a tender age, Bertha could understand the messages being conveyed.

Although Sister Thea spent her formative years in a segregated society, she knew that people of faith and good will could work together to create a more just society. She challenged the Church to embrace cultural diversity and truly live the gospel. In her limited time with us, she sought endlessly to do just that. It is up to us to continue her efforts and those of others. Our large, diverse nation is filled with visionary people who can make a positive change and allow all of God's people to prosper and prevail. Sister Thea challenged us to think of what could be, of how we could embrace additional cultures, not solely the European one. She will be remembered, as Bishop Houck said, for her "recognition of black [culture's contributions] to the Catholic faith."

Xavier University and the Institute for Black Catholic Studies have been tasked with promoting the advancement of five African American sainthood causes. These causes are all known for their devotion to the faith and are in different stages of promotion. They include the Venerable Henriette DeLille, SSF, the founder of the Sisters of the Holy Family in New Orleans in 1842; Servant of God Father Augustus Tolton, a former slave and the first African American priest in the United States, who studied in Rome, as no seminary in the United States would accept him; the Venerable Pierre Toussaint, a freed slave who was born in Saint Dominique (now Haiti), brought to New York, where he became a hairdresser to wealthy patrons, and a renowned philanthropist; Servant of God Mother Mary Elizabeth Lange, OSP, the Cuban-born founder of the Oblate Sisters of Providence, the first religious order for African American women in 1829; and Servant of God Julia Greeley, "Denver's Angel of Charity," a freed slave, who was devoted to her parish, and despite limited means, committed to helping those in need.

Sister Thea was declared a "Servant of God" on May 15, 2018, which initiated the process for her canonization. On November 14, 2018, at their fall general assembly, the U.S. bishops voted unanimously to approve the canonization path for Sister Thea. A few days later, on November 18, 2018, Bishop Joseph R. Kopacz read an edict during a Mass at the Cathedral of St. Peter the Apostle in Jackson. The Diocese of Jackson will lead the investigation into Sister Thea's life. A diocesan commission will conduct interviews and examine her life and writings to determine whether she lived a life of virtue.

Sister Thea taught us what it means to be a universal Church. She believed that black culture could and should be a part of the Church. We can only truly be the Church universal if we are inclusive of our different cultures. Sister Thea understood what it means to be catholic, in light of the four marks of the Catholic Church from the Nicene Creed established by the Council of Nicea in AD 325. The Church is "one, holy, catholic, and apostolic." The Catholic Church is a welcoming place for all seekers. It is up to each of us to make sure that all are welcomed, and that our cultural diversity is represented and embraced. As Sister Thea said, "Do you hear me, Church?"

QUESTIONS FOR REFLECTION AND DISCUSSION

Many subjects are addressed in this book. The life of Sister Thea Bowman, FSPA, raises thought-provoking questions, as well as social and cultural issues. The following questions, grouped by topic, are designed to stimulate individual thought or group discussion. The questions may help you recognize how the present is influenced by past life experiences, such as those experienced by Sister Thea. As you ponder her experiences, consider how some of the struggles she faced are still present today.

GETTING TO KNOW SISTER THEA

1. How much about Sister Thea did you know before reading the book?
2. What did you learn about her?
3. Did anything about her surprise you?
4. What were some things in her childhood that impacted her?

5. Why were the spirituals so important to Sister Thea?

6. What were some major events that affected her life?

SOCIAL ISSUES AND INJUSTICES

1. Given the story of the life of Sister Thea, what do you think it was like for her to suppress her personality and cultural identity at St. Rose Convent? Do you think it was difficult for her to do? How would you feel if you were in Sister Thea's position?

2. How did some of the broader social issues addressed in the book affect Sister Thea?

3. Have you thought about any of these issues before?

4. What was your reaction to the injustices that Sister Thea faced?

5. Have you been introduced to a new perspective after reading the book?

6. Has your perspective on an issue been broadened? If so, how?

HER IMPACT LOCALLY, GLOBALLY, AND CHURCHWIDE

1. What were some of Sister Thea's major accomplishments?

2. What contributions did she make? To whom or what?

3. Was Sister Thea successful? If so, what characteristics did she possess that enabled her to be successful?

4. Where can you see the presence of God in Sister Thea's life?

5. Can you see why she was such an engaging teacher, speaker, and presenter?

THE CALL TO ACTION

1. Can you be Catholic and still retain your cultural identity?

2. Given the current racial climate in the United States, how do you view the timing of Sister Thea's path to canonization?

3. What does the subtitle of the book mean to you?

4. What is the call to action in the book? Is it realistic?

5. Do you feel changed in any way after reading the book? If so, how?

BIBLIOGRAPHY

Albertson, Campbell. "A Lynching Memorial Is Opening. The Country Has Never Seen Anything Like It." *New York Times*, April 25, 2018. https://www.nytimes.com/2018/04/25/us/lynching-memorial-alabama.html.

"An Interview with Mrs. Will Ethel Lofton." Interview by Daisy Greene. Mississippi Department of Archives and History and the Washington County Library System Oral History Project: Greenville and Vicinity, April 15, 1977. www.mdah.ms.gov/arrec/digital_archives/vault/projects/OHtranscripts//AU386_099264.pdf.

"Archives & Special Collections: Honorary Degrees." Marnie and John Burke Memorial Library. Accessed December 22, 2018. https://libguides.shc.edu/archives/honorary.

Barry, John M. *Rising Tide: The Great Mississippi Flood of 1927 and How It Changed America*. New York: Simon & Schuster Paperbacks, 1997.

Bauer, Pam. "Invitation to Sing." *Extension: Magazine of the American Home Missions* 78, no. 7 (January 1984): 5–12.

Beeson, Jeffrey. "U.S. Celebrates 40th Anniversary of Black Studies Programs: MU Observes Black History Month with Acclaimed Author Noliwe Rooks Lecture on Black Studies in the 21st Century." News Bureau University of Missouri, February 3, 2009. https://munews.missouri.edu/news-releases/2009/02.03.09.brunsma.blackstudies.anniversary.php.

Berard, Adrienne. *Water Tossing Boulders: How a Family of Chinese Immigrants Led the First Fight to Desegregate Schools in the Jim Crow South.* Boston: Beacon Press, 2016.

"Bishop Joseph Bernard Brunini." Catholic Diocese of Jackson website. Accessed December 20, 2018. https://jacksondiocese.org/about/diocesan-history/growing-1853-1977/1900s/bishop-joseph-bernard-brunini/.

Blackdeer, Arlene. "Ho-Chunk Nation." Wisconsin First Nations. Accessed September 13, 2018. https://wisconsinfirstnations.org/ho-chunk-nation.

Blinder, Alan. "U.S. Reopens Emmett Till Investigation, Almost 63 Years after His Murder." *New York Times*, July 12, 2018. https://nytimes.com/2018/07/12/us/emmett-till-death-investigation.html.

Bookser-Feister, John. "'I Am Beautiful, You Are Beautiful': Thea Bowman's Ministry of Joy." *St. Anthony Messenger* 93 (July 1985): 29–33.

———. "Teaching Cultural Awareness: A God-Given Survival Skill." *The Cornerstone* (August 1985): 38–42.

———. "We Are All Children of God." *Extension: Magazine of the American Home Missions* 83 (April/May 1989): 24–27.

Bowman, Thea. "Let Us Love One Another." Sister Bowman's Holy Week Reflection. *Mississippi Catholic.* Posted March 20, 2015. Accessed December 4, 2018. https://mississippicatholic.com/2015/03/20/let-us-love-one-another-sister-bowmans-holy-week-reflection/.

———. "Schools Offer Religious, Cultural Variety." *Mississippi Today*, (February 1, 1985): 6–7.

———. "Simple Ways to Work Toward Intercultural Awareness." National Catholic Educational Association: *Momentum* (February 1989): 12.

———. "Spirituality: The Soul of the People." *Tell It Like It Is: A Black Catholic Perspective on Christian Education*, 83–95. Oakland, CA: The National Black Sisters' Conference, 1983.

"Brothers and Sisters to Us," U.S. Catholic Bishops Pastoral Letter on Racism, 1979. www.usccb.org/issues-and-action/cultural-diversity/african-american/brothers-and-sisters-to-us.cfm.

Brown, Joseph A. *A Retreat with Thea Bowman and Bede Abram: Leaning on the Lord*. Cincinnati, OH: St. Anthony Messenger Press, 1997.

Brunsman, Steve. "Faulkner Understood Ole Time Religion." *The Sun Herald*, August 1989, B 1–2.

Catholic News Agency. "Annual Mass Honors 'Rich Cultural Diversity' of Los Angeles Archdiocese." September 12, 2018. https://www.catholicnewsagency.com/news/annual-mass -honors-rich-cultural-diversity-of-los-angeles-archdiocese -50129.

Cepress, Celestine, ed. *Sister Thea Bowman, Shooting Star: Selected Writings and Speeches*. Foreword by Mike Wallace. LaCrosse, WI: Franciscan Sisters of Perpetual Adoration, 1999.

City of Canton, MS website. Accessed November 14, 2018. https:// www.cityofcantonms.com.

"Class Notes." *CUA* Magazine (Fall 1987). Catholic University of America, Washington, DC.

Cobb, Charles E., Jr. *This Nonviolent Stuff'll Get You Killed: How Guns Made the Civil Rights Movement Possible*. New York: Basic Books, 2014.

Condon, Stephanie. "After 148 years, Mississippi Finally Ratifies 13th Amendment, Which Banned Slavery." cbsnews .com, February 18, 2013. https://www.cbsnews.com/ news/after-148-years-mississippi-finally-ratifies-13th -amendment-which-banned-slavery/.

Cone, James H. *The Spirituals and the Blues*. Maryknoll, NY: Orbis Books, 1991.

Cooper, Leesha. "Reading Faulkner Helped Black Nun Understand South." *Jackson Daily News*, July 27, 1986.

Culbreth, Michael. "Culture Cements Bonds of Racial Communication." *The Clarion-Ledger*, January 19, 1985, 17.

Dittmer, John. *Local People: The Struggle for Civil Rights in Mississippi*. Chicago: Urbana/University of Illinois Press, 1994.

Donnelly, Mary Queen. "In Memoriam: Sister Thea Bowman (1937–1990)." *America* (April 28, 1990): 420–21.

"Dr. Theon Bowman, 90, Dies after Illness." *The Commercial Appeal*, December 20, 1984.

Duriga, Joyce, ed. "Art at St. Benedict the African Reflects Experience of Black Catholics." *Chicago Catholic*, June 20, 2018. https://www.chicagocatholic.com/chicagoland/-/article/2018/06/20/art-at-st-benedict-the-african-reflects-experience-of-black-catholi-1.

Dyer, Joseph. "Black Catholics Affect History." *The Daily Mississippian*, The University of Mississippi, February 27, 1998.

———. "Small Steps in Black History Important." *The Daily Mississippian*, The University of Mississippi, February 2, 1999.

Ellington, Cleta. *Christ: The Living Water; The Catholic Church in Mississippi*. Edited by Janna Avalon. Jackson: Mississippi Today, 1989.

"Figures of Faith Preside over Birder Hall." St. Norbert College Magazine. Accessed November 30, 2018. https://www.snc.edu/magazine/2014fallwinter/birderstatues.html.

Gervais, Kathryn. "Sr. Thea Bowman Dies, Was Beloved Evangelist." *Catholic Standard* 40 (April 5, 1990): 1, 17.

Giaimo, Donna William. "Sr. Thea Bowman: A Song in Her Soul." *The Family* (February 1989): 20–22.

"Give Me That Ole Time Religion." *Mississippi Today*, Jackson, MS, December 5, 1986.

Gschwind, Mary Ann. "Bowman, Sister Thea (1937–1990)." In *Black Women in America: An Historical Encyclopedia*, 155–57. Edited by Darlene Clark Hine. Vol. 1, A–L. Brooklyn, NY: Carlson Publishing, 1993.

"Hallelujah Singers." *La Crosse Tribune*, December 3, 1977, 17. https://www.newspapers.com/clip/8139156/hallelujah_singers_and_innovative_arts/.

Hansen, Nathan. "Sociologist Discusses La Crosse's History as a 'Sundown Town.'" *La Crosse Tribune*, October 28, 2016. https://lacrossetribune.com/news/local/sociologist-discusses-la-crosse-s-history-as-a-sundown-town/article_309535b3-867a-55c6-8f56-c291ed932bfb.html.

Healy, Michael. "Lessons in Lyrical Voices from 'an Old Folks' Child." *Common Life* 1, no. 1 (Spring 1990): 4–10.

"History of Lynchings." National Association for the Advancement of Colored People (NAACP). Accessed December 30,

2018. https://naacp.org/history-of-lynchings/.holyrosary indianmission.com (accessed August 8, 2018).

"I Am a Part of All That I Have Met: An Interview with Sister Thea Bowman." *FSPA Perspectives* 3, no. 2 (Spring 1988): 3–4.

Johnson, Thomas J. "Fannie Lou Hamer Dies; Left Farm to Learn Struggle for Civil Rights." *New York Times*, March 15, 1977. https://www.nytimes.com/1977/03/15/archives/fannie-lou-hamer-dies-left-farm-to-lead-struggle-for-civil-rights.html.

Koontz, Christian, ed. *Thea Bowman: Handing on Her Legacy*. New York: Sheed & Ward, 1991.

Loewen, James W. "Showing La Crosse in Wisconsin." Accessed September 26, 2018. https://sundown.tougaloo.edu/sundowntownsshow.php?id=2540.

———. *Sundown Towns: A Hidden Dimension of American Racism*. New York: New Press, 2005.

Long, Robert Lee. "C. O. Chinn Dead at 80, Civil Rights Activist." *Madison County Journal* (July 22, 1999): 1–2.

Ludwig, M. Mileta. *A Chapter of Franciscan History: The Sisters of the Third Order of Saint Francis of Perpetual Adoration, 1849–1949*. New York: Bookman Associates, 1950.

"Making a Joyful Noise: The Story of Thea Bowman, FSPA." *Rising Dawn*, The Archdiocese of Saint Paul and Minneapolis, Commission on Women (Spring 1994): 10, 11.

Masur, Louis P. "Why It Took a Century to Pass an Anti-Lynching Law." *The Washington Post*, December 28, 2018. https://www.washingtonpost.com/outlook/2018/12/28/why-it-took-century-pass-an-anti-lynching-law/?utm_term=.f5201a66cf19.

McGovern, Mary E. "Indian Literature Topic: Native American Culture." *Lumen*, Viterbo College, 20, no. 6 (February 14, 1975): 1.

McGrath, Michael O'Neill. *This Little Light of Mine: Lessons in Living from Sister Thea Bowman*. Maryknoll, NY: Orbis Books, 2008.

Minor, W. F. "Priest Leads Flock to Church: City's Block on Building Said Cause of Action." *Times-Picayune*, May 25, 1965.

Mission Civil Rights Project. "House of Sister Thea Bowman." Accessed December 20, 2018. https://mscivilrightsproject .org/counties/madison/.

Moore, Cecilia. "Black Catholic Pilgrims and Pioneers: African American Catholic History." *Catechist* 34, no. 5 (February 2001): 50–55.

Ms.gov. "About Mississippi." Accessed December 20, 2018. https://www.ms.gov/Visitors/About_Mississippi.

Muldoon, Tim. "King Anniversary Recalls Bishop's Desegregation Efforts in Mississippi." *Catholic News Service*, April 6, 2018. https://www.catholicnews.com/services/englishnews/ 2018/king-anniversary-recalls-bishops-desegregation -efforts-in-mississippi.cfm.

Namorato, Michael V. *The Catholic Church in Mississippi, 1911–1984: A History*. Westport, CT: Greenwood Press, 1998.

————. "Joseph Brunini," *Mississippi Encyclopedia*. Oxford, MS: Center for the Study of Southern Culture, University of Mississippi. Accessed November 3, 2018. https:// mississippiencyclopedia.org/entires/joseph-brunini/.

"Native Americans to Stage Pow-Wow." *Lumen*, Viterbo College (April 20, 1975): 3.

"Negroes Want a Church but…" *Times-Review*, June 4, 1965.

Newton, Brother Dennis. "St. Augustine's Seminary." Accessed November 27, 2018. www.svdsouth.com/st.-augustine -seminary.html.

Njemanze, Beatrice. "Sister Thea Bowman Touches Her African Roots." *Mississippi Today* (September 13, 1985): 7.

"Open Wide Our Hearts: The Enduring Call to Love; A Pastoral Letter against Racism." USCCB, November 14, 2018, 1–32. www .usccb.org/issues-and-action/human-life-and-dignity/ racism/upload/open-wide-our-own-hearts.pdf.

Padgett, John B. "William Faulkner." The Mississippi Writers Page. Department of English, The University of Missis- sippi, November 9, 2015. mwp.olemiss.edu//dir/faulkner _william/.

Pilgrim, David. "What Was Jim Crow." Jim Crow Museum, Ferris State University, Big Rapids, MI. Accessed December 15, 2018. https://ferris.edu/jimcrow/what.htm.

Ransburg, Jo Ann. "Thea's Light Shines, and Shines and Shines." *Lumen*, Viterbo College 23, no. 16 (February 22, 1978): 5.

Rayborn, Lela. "A Brief History of Mississippi State Federation of Colored Women's Clubs, Incorporated." MSFCWC, July 2005. http://www.msfcwcinc.org/history.htm.

Ruane, Michael E. "Fifty Years Ago Some Called D.C. 'the Colored Man's Paradise.' Then Paradise Erupted." *The Washington Post*, March 26, 2018. https://www.washingtonpost.com/local/fifty-years-ago-some-called-dc-the-colored-mans-paradise-then-paradise-erupted/2018/03/22/6ae9ec1c-208e-11e8-94da-ebf9d112159c_story.html.

Rubin, Susan Goldman. *Freedom Summer: The 1964 Struggle for Civil Rights in Mississippi*. New York: Holiday House, 2014.

"S. 2854-114th Congress (2015–2016): Emmett Till Unsolved Civil Rights Crimes Reauthorization Act of 2016." Accessed December 22, 2018. https://www.congress.gov/bill/114th-congress/senate-bill/2854.

Sacred Heart University. "Commencement 1989." Accessed September 26, 2019. https://digitalcommons.sacredheart.edu/univpub_commencement/19/.

"Saint Benedict the Moor." Roman Catholic Saints. Accessed December 29, 2018. https://www.roman-catholic-saints.com/st-benedict-the-moor.html.

Saint Joseph's University. "Annual Lecture Series Honors Sister Thea Bowman, F.S.P.A., Scholar and Social Justice Worker." Accessed February 11, 2018. https://www.sju.edu/news-events/news/annual-lecture-series-honors-sister-thea-bowman-fspa-scholar-and-social-justice.

"Saint Thea." Accessed December 12, 2018. http://thenunsgarden.org/saint-thea.php.

"The Salt Wagon Story." Nashville, TN: Meharry Medical College. www.mmc.edu/about/salt-wagon-story.html (accessed September 25, 2018).

"Salt Wagon Student Run Free Health Clinic." Meharry Medical College, Nashville, TN. Accessed October 2, 2018. https://home.mmc.edu/community-initiatives/salt-wagon-student-run-free-health-clinic.

"Shotgun Houses." Accessed December 22, 2018. http://
northbysouth.kenyon.edu/2002/Space/shot2.htm.

"Sister Thea Foundation Aids Black Children." *Mississippi Today*,
August 18, 1989, 4.

Smith, Charlene. "Thea-logy: Memories of Thea Bowman." *U.S.
Catholic* 75, no. 3 (March 2010): 47–48.

Smith, Charlene, and John Feister. *Thea's Song: The Life of Thea
Bowman*. Maryknoll, New York: Orbis Books, 2009.

Smith, Maureen. "Edict Opens Sister Thea Bowman's Cause."
Mississippi Catholic, December 12, 2018. https://
mississippicatholic.com/2018/12/12/edict-opens-sister
-thea-bowmans-cause.

————. "Foundation to Honor Sister Thea Bowman, Other
Women of Courage." *Mississippi Catholic*. Accessed December 23, 2018. www.mississippicatholic.com/tag/sister
-thea-bowman/.

"St. Cloud Girl Reports on Difficulties in the South." *St. Cloud Vis-
itor* 54 (June 6, 1965): 7.

Stockman, Dan. "Sr. Thea Bowman Expected to Be Approved for
Sainthood Path." Global Sisters Report. *National Catholic
Reporter*, August 2, 2018. https://www.globalsistersreport
.org/news/trends/sr-thea-bowman-expected-be
-approved-sainthood-path-55244.

"The Story behind the Name Activity—Greenville Arts Partnership."
Accessed February 19, 2017. https://greenvilleartspartner
ship.files.wordpress.com/2010/12the-story-behind-the
-name-activity.pdf.

Sucre, Richard. "The Great White Plague: The Culture of
Death and the Tuberculosis Sanatorium." Accessed
December 27, 2018. http://www.faculty.virginia.edu/
blueridgesanatorium/death.htm.

Sugre, Thomas J. "Driving While Black: The Car and Race Rela-
tions in Modern America." Accessed December 27, 2018.
www.autolife.umd.umich.edu/Race/R_Casestudy/R
_Casestudy2.htm.

Taylor, Fabvienen, interviewer. "Lord, Let Me Live till I Die." *Praying*. *National Catholic Reporter* 30 (November–December 1989): 19–22.

————. "Mourners Celebrate Sister Bowman." *Mississippi Today*, April 8, 1990, 16.

Townsend, Jacinda. "How the Green Book Helped African-American Tourists Navigate a Segregated Nation." *Smithsonian Magazine*, April 2016. https://www.smithsonianmag.com/Smithsonian-institution/history-green-book-african-american-travelers-180958506/.

Traverso, V. M. "How a Chicago Parish Designed a Church Based on Its People." *Aleteia*, July 9, 2018. https://aleteia.org/2018/07/09/how-a-chicago-parish-designed-a-church-based-on-its-people/.

"Trusting the Prophetic Call." *Creation Magazine* 5, no. 4 (November/December 1989): 19–21.

Tyson, Timothy B. *The Blood of Emmett Till*. New York: Simon & Schuster, 2017.

"U.S. Catholic Honors Sister Thea Bowman." *Mississippi Today*, May 12, 1989, 11.

"'What We Have Seen and Heard': A Pastoral Letter on Evangelization from the Black Catholic Bishops of the United States." USCCB, September 9, 1984, 1–40. www.usccb.org/issues-and-action/cultural-diversity/african-american/resources/upload/what-we-have-seen-and-heard.pdf.

"Who We Are." Archdiocese of Washington. Accessed December 6, 2018. https://adw.org/about-us/who-we-are/.

Wilkerson, Isabel. *The Warmth of Other Suns: The Epic Story of America's Great Migration*. New York: Random House, 2010.

AUDIOVISUALS

Almost Home: Living with Suffering and Dying. Liguori, MO: Liguori Publishing Co., 1989. Audiocassette.

Sister Thea: Her Own Story. Belleville, IL: Oblate Media and Communications, 1991. Videocassette.

UNPUBLISHED SOURCES

Bowman, Thea. May 25, 1989, letter to friends and colleagues.
————. "Assembly Programs."
————. November 26, 1989, letter to friends and colleagues.
————. "That All May Be One: A Multi-Cultural Awareness Day."
"A Brief History of Holy Child Jesus Mission at Canton, Mississippi," 1–5.
Gerow, R. O., Most Reverend. May 22, 1965, letter to Rev. Patrick Moran, pastor, Sacred Heart Church, Canton, MS.
"Holy Child Jesus Catholic Church, Canton, Mississippi, 35th Anniversary, 1947–1982."
Mabus, Ray, Governor of Mississippi. April 2, 1990, letter to Rev. Jim Throwbridge, pastor, Holy Child Jesus Church, Canton, MS.
Mikschl, Rev. Luke, ST. Unsigned letter "Fellow Citizens of Canton," Canton, MS.
Reich, Warren, M.S.SS.T. "Saga of Frog Hollow," circa 1953.
Sweeney, Mary A. "Early Canton Days," June 1978.
Wiesneske, Sister Sarah, FSPA, and Sister Vera Marie Andrle, FSPA. "Holy Child Jesus School, 1948–1978," iv.